KU-255-073

THE GDR

A background to East German studies
by
Derek Lewis
with Sabina Brumsack

WITHDRAWN
University of
Reading Library

BULMERSHE LIBRARY

95 0209489 6

Lochee Publications 1988

All rights reserved. No part of this publication may be reproduced, stored in a retrieval system, or transmitted, in any form or by any means, electronic, mechanical, photocopying, recording or otherwise, without the prior permission of the publisher.

ISBN 0 947584 55 2

LOCHEE PUBLICATIONS LTD.
Oak Villa
New Alyth
Blairgowrie
PH11 8NN
Scotland

© Copyright Lochee Publications Ltd. 1988

THE GDR

An Introduction

By Derek Lewis
with Sabine Brumsack

BULMERSHE COLLEGE OF HIGHER EDUCATION	
CLASS No.	ACCESS No.
943.1087	209489

Table of Contents

Chapter 1   1
INTRODUCTION

Chapter 2   3
COMMUNISM - A BRIEF HISTORY

2.1 Marxian Socialism in More Detail   4

2.2 From Marx to Lenin and Stalin   6

Chapter 3   9
THE END OF THE WAR

3.1 Zones of Occupation   9

3.2 New Parties   11

3.3 The Anti-Fascist Block   12

3.4 Central Administrations   13

3.5 Land and Industrial Reform   13

3.6 Founding of the SED   14

3.7 The Elections of 1946   16

3.8 The SED Tightens its Control   17

3.9 The People's Congress   17

3.10 New Parties   18

3.11 The New Type of Party   19

Chapter 4   20
FROM FOUNDATION TO THE PRESENT

4.1 The National Front of Democratic Germany   20

4.2 The Economy and the First Five Year Plan   21

4.3 The "New Course" (1953)   23

4.4 The Uprising of 17th June 1953   24

4.5 The New Course Continued .... and Ended   25

4.6 Sovereignty   26

4.7 The State of the Nation in 1955   27

4.8 Destalinisation Revisited   28

4.9 Opposition and the Harich Group   29

4.10 Neutralisation of Opposition and the "Completion 30
of Socialism"

4.11 Collectivisation of Agriculture   32

4.12 The State Council (Staatsrat) and Increased   33
Unpopularity of the SED

4.13 The Crisis of 1961 and the Berlin Wall   33

4.14 After the Wall   35

4.15 The New Economic System (1963) and the Age   36
of Socialism

4.16 The Constitution of 1968   37

4.17 The Prague Spring of 1968   38

4.18 A New Confidence: the Science of Socialism?   39

4.19 Relations with the Federal Republic: The Long   41

Road to Ostpolitik

4.20 Stalin's Note of 1952   41

4.21 The Long Freeze and the "Two States" Theory   42

4.22 The Open Letter of 1966   44

4.23 Willy Brandt's Ostpolitik   45

4.24 Treaties   46

4.25 From Ulbricht to Honecker   49

4.26 Changes in Apparatus and Constitution   50

4.27 Economic Upswing and a New Social Policy   51

4.28 Coping with Mounting Opposition and Economic   53
      Stagnation

4.29 Relations with the West in the Early 1980s   55

Chapter 5   59
THE APPARATUS

5.1 The People's Chamber (Volkskammer)   60

5.2 The Council of State   61

5.3 The Council of Ministers   61

5.4 "Bezirke" and "Kreise"   62

5.5 The SED Party Organisation   64

5.6 Congress   64

5.7 The Central Committee   65

5.8 The Politbureau   65

5.9 The Secretariat of the Central Committee   66

5.10 The Control Commission 67

5.11 Membership 67

Chapter 6 69
GEOGRAPHY AND NATURAL RESOURCES

6.1 Boundaries 69

6.2 Landforms 72

6.3 Climate 76

6.4 Vegetation 76

6.5 Agriculture 77

6.6 Population and Resources 79

6.7 Industry 80

6.8 Private Enterprise 83

6.9 Communications 84

6.10 Roads 85

6.11 Waterways 86

6.12 Ports 86

Chapter 7 88
ECONOMIC PLANNING

7.1 Who is involved in the planning process? 89

7.2 What types of plan exist? 90

7.3 Plans since 1948 92

7.4 How Effective are the Plans? 96

Chapter 8   98
EDUCATION IN THE GDR

8.1 Historical Development   98

8.2 Policy and Aims   101

8.3 The Education Act of 1965   103

8.4 Career Selection   104

8.5 Education and the State   105

8.6 Pre-School Education   107

8.7 The Ten-Year General Polytechnical Upper School   107

8.8 Military Education   109

8.9 The Extended Upper School   110

8.10 Polytechnical Education in more Detail   112

8.11 Special Schools   114

8.12 Vocational Training   115

8.13 Outside School Hours   117

8.14 An Assessment of the Education System   120

Chapter 9   123
CULTURAL POLICY

9.1 The Early Years   123

9.2 The Bitterfeld Way and Social Realism   125

9.3 Theatre, Music, Opera, Film   127

9.4 1965: An Ideological Winter   128

9.5 1971: A Thaw in Cultural Policy   132

9.6 1976: An End to Flexibility   133

9.7 The Biermann-Protest   134

9.8 Cultural Opportunites for the People   136

9.9 The Cultural Underground   137

9.10 A Note on Dissidence   138

Chapter 10   142
MEDIA IN THE GDR

10.1 The Ideological Basis   143

10.2 History and Organisation of the Press   147

10.3 Structure of the Press   151

10.4 Journalists   154

10.5 Radio   155

10.6 Television   158

10.7 Conclusion   161

Chapter 11   163
A REVIEW OF RESOURCES

CHAPTER 1
INTRODUCTION

This book provides an introductory study to important aspects of life, history and culture in the German Democratic Republic. It is aimed at sixth-formers, undergraduates and others with a serious interest in this country, which has emerged within the last decade from relative obscurity to assume a significant place in German studies in schools and universities.

There are several reasons for such a renaissance of attention. For one thing, a nation which has become the most efficient and productive economic unit in the Eastern Block after suffering the compounded problems of war-damage, Soviet reparations and chronic shortages of basic resources - not to mention the imposition of an ill-developed model of economic planning that was thoroughly alien to its sophisticated workforce - merits much greater interest than the usual Soviet satellite. Although post-war attention focussed on the "miracle" of West German economic recovery, the resurrection of the GDR as a viable economic entity in the prevailing circumstances represents in many respects a more genuine "wonder". It is known that East Germany has provided "laboratory conditions" for the Soviet system in a technologically more advanced society than anywhere else in the communist world, although whether the German "experiment" will influence the international development of socialism is not yet clear. And, of course, the GDR has traditionally suffered from unfavourable comparisons with the more prosperous Federal Republic and doubts about its long-term viability in view of the West Germans' claim - not so strongly advanced nowadays but still not entirely renounced - to represent Germans on both sides of the border. Thus, East German studies suffered from undue neglect for too long and for reasons which were perhaps too artificial inasmuch as they were rooted more in prejudgment than in knowledge.

A further possible reason for interest in the GDR may have more to do with a certain lessening of confidence in the western world in its own economic system, especially in the 1980s with its problems of recession and challenges to its international hegemony, both material and moral. At the time of writing it is too early to predict what, if anything, will emerge from the dramatic initiatives on arms limitations which emanated from the new Soviet leadership during the latter half of the 1980s or from the tentative policy of internal "openness", but it is certainly true that these developments have led to a public re-evaluation of the western powers commitment to nuclear disarmament (as opposed to lip-service) and to a weakening of the traditional friend-foe mould into which most westerners' public perception of the communist bloc had degenerated. While East Germany as such has no active role in these events, it may well be assumed that it is likely to profit in the long run from a closer, more objective and less self-assured scrutiny from western countries.

In a volume of this size many areas must remain unmentioned, but it is hoped that the approach adopted and the aspects covered will provide a sound factual basis for an understanding of the GDR's difficult past, its relationship with West Germany, the present organisation of the state and its most significant institutions as well as basic geography and cultural policy. While the author is not a Marxist and must remain sceptical of such a closed ideological system, an honest effort has been made to present the intentions, achievements and failures of East German communism in a straightforward but sympathetic light in order to facilitate an understanding of the GDR for young western readers. The general introduction to communism will not satisfy the political scientist, the assessment of economic planning will not embrace enough factors for the economist and the literary specialist will be seeking more nuances than he will find here, but the reader approaching the subject of East Germany for the first time may discover in this book an informative springboard for further research.

CHAPTER 2
COMMUNISM - A BRIEF HISTORY

East Germany is a communist state and as such has its roots in a political philosophy dating back into the early 19th century. Let us look briefly at the origins of communism and establish what the term itself means.

Rapid industrialisation from the 18th century onwards produced - especially in Britain - the doctrine of "economic liberalism" or "laissez faire". The apparent centrepiece of this doctrine was the freedom of the individual, but for the emerging entrepeneurs of the industrial revolution this freedom was interpreted in a very specific way to mean no government interference in trade, working conditions or wage levels, no monopolies (especially state regulated ones) or trade unions, which were considered to violate the freedom of contract between individuals who, in this case, were the employer and his employee. Between 1800 and 1860 most restrictions in the UK on private trade and industry - these had often evolved over several centuries of mercantile activity - were actually repealed or lifted in the name of "laissez faire". A small class grew extremely wealthy and there was a general belief that Britain, as the foremost proponent of economic liberalism, was prospering precisely because she was following the "laws of nature" in dispensing with man-made restrictions.

Either in spite or because of the theory unrestricted industrial practices produced wide scale mass poverty and human exploitation and critics of social conditions in Britain and the continent were soon to hand although small in number and influence. "Socialism" was a term given to more than one such reactive movemement proposing changes in social organisation. "Utopian Socialism", for example, as advanced by Charles Fourier in France, advocated self-sufficient co-operatives producing their own food and materials. The "Stage Socialism" of Louis Blanc, on the other hand, suggested similar communities but promoted and guaranteed by the state itself.

In 1848, in their "Communist Manifesto", two Germans, Karl Marx and Friedrich Engels formulated proposals for a new kind of society called "Marxian Socialism" or "Communism". Basically this envisaged the emerging social class of workers growing in number and discipline and seizing power from the ruling industrialist class by revolution - the revolution would not necessarily be of a violent nature, but this would depend on the degree of autocracy in individual states. What was novel in this view was the vivid formulation of class warfare and the vision of the entire state apparatus overthrown by the work-hardened, organised proletariat finally assuming its rightful control of the means of economic production (factories, farms, businesses, etc).

From 1870 onwards Marxian Socialism became the dominant voice of protest against industrial capitalism and even began to unnerve governments. Socialist parties were founded in Europe, trade unions formed - even MPs returned to parliaments - and an international federation, the Socialist International, was established.

2.1 Marxian Socialism in More Detail

Karl Marx was the first person to work out a thorough philosophy of socialism. This philosophy was based on a systematic study of economic history which he undertook during his prolonged exile in London after he had fled his native Germany on account of his revolutionary activities.

The ideological principles of Marxian Socialism can be summarised as follows:

(1) History is determined by material and economic factors - indeed not only the course of historical events but also institutions (e.g. government and law), culture, art and religion are created and moulded by the

determinism of purely economic forces. The most powerful of these is the ownership of the means of production of food and goods: this constitutes an "economic relation" which leads to a conflict between economic classes. Just as the bourgeoisie fought against the feudal nobility for control of the means of production (and ultimate wealth), so the working masses exploited by the new controllers of capital resources inevitably confront their new overlords.

(2) Marx predicted that the control of money or capital by the bourgeoisie would follow a pattern. Big businesses would successively take over smaller ones leading to a concentration of wealth in the hands of a tiny minority of very rich "monopoly capitalists". In this situation, of course, the army of dependent workers would vastly increase, providing the right context for an uprising and a seizure of power. Such a revolution might take place peacefully through the ballot box in democratic countries (e.g. Britain), but would entail violent and bitter struggle where the capitalists controlled the police, the armed forces, the media and the legal system.

(3) After a brief period in which the workers themselves imposed their rule - the so-called "dictatorship of the proletariat" - the class struggle would end and people would enjoy the benefits of living in a classless, socialist society where no individual class monopolised economic wealth to the detriment of others.

During the late 19th century socialism fragmented into various movements, the main difference being the commitment to violent revolution. Those who felt that the ideals of social equality and equitable distribution of wealth could and should be achieved by peaceful reform and compromise with existing power structures formed moderate left-wing parties such as the British Labour Party and the Social Democratic Party in Germany. Communism as such came to be associated with "pure" Marxism, as described above, and with its extreme analyses and solutions.

2.2 From Marx to Lenin and Stalin

The next major figure to form modern communism is Nikolai Lenin who came to power in Russia in 1917. In this year events in Russia were in turmoil. Incompetently led in a disastrous war against Germany, a hungry and demoralised people had overthrown the Tsar and replaced him with at first a provisional government and then a democratically elected assembly. Neither had much chance, however, in the face of the crushing demands of continuing effective resistance against Germany and of Lenin's small but highly organised and determined communist party. Assisted by the Germans themselves, Lenin seized power, concluded peace with Germany (which was now free to concentrate on its own beleagured Western Front), and proceeded to create Europe's first communist state. The circumstances of the communist revolution may not have been quite how Marx envisaged them or even in the country of his choice, but the result was clear enough: a dictatorship of the party of the proletariat which tolerated no domestic opposition and which the bulk of peasants and workers supported for fear of return to the days of the old landowners and corrupt nobility.

Lenin's government survived foreign interference, civil war and famine. With dedicated ruthlessness and at the cost of millions of lives, opponents were eradicated, land and industry taken out of private hands, and a system of government established ranging from local party cells in factories, offices and villages to a National Party Congress which elected a Central Committee with a supremely powerful "Political Bureau" of nine members.

Lenin's contribution to the march of communism was his conception of a "New Type Party", which the Communist Party of the Soviet Union came to embody under his leadership. In the eyes of many effectively divorcing itself from the original egalitarian ideals of Marxian socialism, the party turned itself into a very highly organised, hierarchically controlled and tightly disciplined machine. It now understood itself as the "vanguard" of socialism, which meant that, instead of truly representing the interests of the workers as they might perhaps have conceived them themselves, the communist party assumed the role of leadership and of educating the working masses towards predefined ideological goals. It swiftly became a starkly elitist party, governed by a relatively tiny group of individuals presiding above a large and bureaucratic apparatus, and it assumed characteristics of a dictatorship. In defence of the new type party it could be claimed that the prospects of communism surviving as a leading political force and of achieving universal socialism would have been negligible without a programme of internal regimentation and concentration of power along these lines. Lenin wrote extensively about the role, organisation and future of the communist party, so that Marxism-Leninism has the status of sound theory in communist countries, with Lenin credited with having given the ideals of Marx a basis for practical realisation.

The vanguard role of the organised communist party was clearly formulated by the future East German party leader, Walter Ulbricht, who wrote in typically colourless prose that "The Marxist-Leninist party constitutes the most advanced form of organization among all the organizations of the working class. It embodies the alliance between the vanguard of the working class and the rank and file of the working class and the working people." He went on to stress that an organisation of this kind could only fulfil its tasks with "unified party statutes, a unified party discipline and a unified party leadership, which mediates the line of party policy to the masses through its central newspaper. Only a militant party of this type is capable, at the present period, of conducting the struggle and of sweeping aside all obstacles on the way towards our goal - the capture of working class power. ... If the party wants to fulfil its task of the vanguard, it must be distinct from the broad masses in the composition of its membership and in its ideological level."

Lenin's successor in 1924, Joseph Stalin, continued the tradition of dictatorship. Liquidation of opponents (or even peasants - the "kulaks" - who had prospered under Lenin's "New Economic Policy" which had introduced in 1921 some degree of private economic activity and land ownership in order to counteract an imminent national economic collapse) alternated with collectivisation of agriculture, five year economic development plans, and mass educational programmes. By the late 1930's the Soviet Union had become a major industrial power and sole example of uncompromising communism in practice, although it had cut itself off from the wider and more moderate international socialist movement.

Events were now abruptly overshadowed by the Second World War and by Nazi Germany's decision to invade Russia in 1941. After possibly the bitterest military struggle in human history, however, the Russians drove back the invaders and, by 1945, found themselves in effective possession of most of Central and Eastern Europe, including Eastern Germany. Thus the stage was set for Soviet style communism to directly influence the lives of millions of German citizens. For the first time the Soviet Union had played a part in subjugating a superior industrial power. The eventual transplantation of a variety of communism which had evolved in one of the politically and economically most backward states of Europe onto a section of the highly developed former German Reich provided fascinating "laboratory" conditions for a unique social experiment over which the Germans themselves, of course, had little control.

CHAPTER 3
THE END OF THE WAR

3.1 Zones of Occupation

The immediate future of defeated Nazi Germany in 1945 was the subject of a conference of the victorious allies, including the Soviet Union, which was held in Potsdam, a suburb of the former imperial capital, Berlin. The USA, UK, France and the USSR divided Germany into zones of occupation in which each ally exercised virtual sovereign control (the city of Berlin was similarly divided into sectors on the principle that no single victor should have control over the capital). Although the allies met in the so-called Allied Control Council in order to administer Germany as a whole and to preserve its national identity, the decision to set up zones was a fateful one that was subsequently to result in the more or less permanent division of the country into a western half incorporated into NATO (the Federal Republic) and an eastern half which is now firmly integrated into the communist bloc (the German Democratic Republic).

The process by which zonal divisions became permanent state boundaries is a long and complex one - and the subject of differing interpretations between East and West - but before outlining briefly the major stages along this road, let us look more closely at Soviet policy towards its German occupees directly after the war.

Firstly, the Russians, having suffered greviously during the war (20 million of their citizens perished), were - like their western allies - first and foremost concerned that Germany should no longer be in a position to wage a war of territorial aggrandisement. To this end Germany's military capability, its armaments industry, and all vestiges of National Socialism were to be destroyed. Long before the end of hostilities, however, the Russian leader, Stalin, officially distanced himself from all plans advanced by the British and Americans to turn Germany into a purely agricultural country and showed little interest in a permanent division of the Reich. Actually the Russians' prime aim came increasingly to lie in extracting maximum possible reparations for their own extensive war damage and since the raw materials and industrial plant for this would have to come substantially from western zones of occupation, e.g. the Ruhrgebiet in the British zone, then the best way of achieving this goal was through an agreed and concerted policy with the allies treating Germany as an entity.

A long term ambition of the Soviets was no doubt the installation of their own system, but they did not proceed overtly with this in the immediate period after the war to any greater degree than either the British or the Americans who also brought in their "own" people to run things.

In Moscow the Russians had already been preparing a team of German communists for some time before the end of the war to assume a leading role in a future Soviet administered German area. These were members of the German Communist Party (<u>Kommunistische Partei Deutschlands</u> or KPD) which had thrived in a Germany severely affected by the world depression before Hitler's take over in 1933 and had been closely modelled on the Soviet Communist Party in its strict organisation and adherence to Soviet views. Thousands of its members had, moreover been tortured, imprisoned and murdered by the Nazis and it retains to this day a traumatic group memory of those times. One week before the Nazi capitulation, then, a group of leading German communists was flown into Russian-occupied Berlin under the leadership of Walter Ulbricht, who was entrusted with the task of assisting the Soviet authorities. Similar groups were despatched to the provinces of Saxony and Mecklenburg-Pommerania. German communists received key positions, although political parties as such - even the KPD - were not yet admitted. The priority of the Soviet authorities was to establish functioning local administrations of basic services under their strict control and even the spontaneous pro-communist anti-fascist committees which proliferated immediately after the war were swiftly wound up and discouraged: in Ulbricht's words: "It must look democratic, but we have got to have everything in our control"[2] The instrument of Soviet governership of their zone was the so-called SMAD (Sowjetische Administration in Deutschland). The SMAD was set up in June 1945, ruled the zone by a series of issued decrees ("Befehle") and was directly controlled by the Political Bureau in Moscow and by Stalin himself, who took a personal interest in German affairs. Probably the most influential department of SMAD was that for Propaganda (later called Information), consisting of over 150 officers who in time controlled the media and influenced the establishment and control of trade unions, mass organisations and political parties. As a highly organised, centralised and all-powerful apparatus with a monopoly on resources, control of information, and in a position to hand out privileges, the SMAD acted quickly and effectively to re-organise all aspects of life in the zone, from education to transport, industry and agriculture. Above all it placed trusted communists in essential posts thereby presenting the allies with a ready made Soviet-orientated machinery of zonal administration.

3.2 New Parties

The Russians were the first to allow political parties and trade unions to re-form in Germany (decree number two of the SMAD) and that they encouraged the historical democratic parties of the pre-Hitler period was a signal to the western allies that they did not plan a wholesale communist takeover. The permitted parties reflected a western style pluralism of interests. In order of appearance in June/July 1945 they were:

1. The Communist Party (KPD): Chairman Wilhelm Pieck.

2. The Social Democratic Party (Sozialdemokratische Partei Deutschlands or SPD): Chairman Otto Grotewohl.

3. The Christian Democratic Union (Christlich-Demokratische Union or CDU): Chairman Andreas Hermes. The core of this party lay in individuals of religious and conservative background, although the Soviet authorities did not anticipate much support for what had been formerly a catholic interest group in the mainly protestant eastern zone.

4. The Liberal Democratic Party (Liberal-Demokratische Partei or LDP): Chairman Waldemar Koch. The LDP appealed to former middle class business interests in its call for the retention of private ownership, free enterprise and a non-political judiciary and civil service.

In keeping with the gradualist approach the KPD - under instructions from Moscow - distanced itself in its manifesto from a revolutionary, Soviet-style approach which would have entailed advocating the overthrow of existing traditional institutions. Even free trade and private enterprise were guaranteed. So, despite, its closeness to the Soviet Union, the KPD under Soviet direction increased its membership by broadening its appeal and hence avoided widespread alienation of the masses. It consolidated its organisation and personnel, and then, and only then, from a position of internal strength, contemplated merging with and effectively taking over the Social Democratic Party to create a new unified workers party, the Socialist Unity Party (Sozialistische Einheitspartei Deutschlands or SED) in April 1946.

3.3 The Anti-Fascist Block

Before this, however, a new concept in German politics emerged with the "Anti-Fascist Block" (or "United Front of Anti-Fascist Democratic Parties") which was set up with branches throughout the Eastern Zone. Instead of competing with one another the four parties agreed to confer and act in unison on key issues, in particular the eradication of of Nazism, the re-establishment of democracy and the rebuilding of Germany. Behind the attractive formulae, however, the United Front was to conceal basic differences as to how and with what policies these aims should be realised. With its privileged position vis-a-vis the occupying power the KPD was able to exploit the Block as a tool to curb the parties' independence and exert far greater control behind the scenes than it appeared to possess at face value.

3.4 Central Administrations

July 1945 saw also the swift setting up of so-called Central Administrations in Berlin responsible throughout the Eastern Zone for transport, communications, energy, trade, industry, supply, agriculture, finance, work and welfare, general education, justice, and health. They had no powers as such, but functioned entirely as organs of the SMAD, who were intent on a rapid return to normality after the disruption of the war, on placing reliable communists in key positions in the running of the country and in presenting the western allies with "accomplished facts" in any future re-organisation in the direction of a united Germany. Each Central Administration was headed by a President, invariably a KPD member or at least in the pocket of the communists (the staffing of these Central Administrations led to considerable acrimony on the part of the other parties but these were in no position to argue with the SMAD).

3.5 Land and Industrial Reform

The old Junker class of landed aristocracy, who possessed vast estates in the east of the country and had traditionally been a barrier to social and political progress in pre-war Germany, became an immediate target for disappropriation under the occupying power. In fact all political parties agreed unanimously that the Junkers should be stripped of their land - which took place in September 1945 - but the CDU incurred the displeasure of the Russians by trying to insist that it should be accompanied by compensation. The land was distributed among half a million farm workers, landless peasants and workers and about one third given over to the community. The Land Reform was not a specifically communist measure, nor did it constitute a complete takeover of private land by the state: indeed many small landowners were actually created overnight.

The nationalisation of heavy industry was a more radical measure, preceded by the nationalisation of banks in July 1945. Already, concerns formerly owned by the Nazis and by the army had been confiscated and the SMAD held a carefully prepared referendum in the state of Saxony on the 30th June 1946 to enable the people to decide whether businesses and firms which had been in the hands of Nazi "war criminals" or had served their "war interests" should be taken over by the state without compensation. On a vote of 77% in favour, this measure was indeed adopted for Saxony and subsequently for the rest of the Eastern Zone (without further referenda). The CDU and LDP fiercely - and vainly - resisted the measure, which placed 40% of industrial production in state ownership and paved the way for major economic re-organisation along communist lines.

3.6 Founding of the SED

The SPD was the largest single political party in the Eastern Zone and possessed the highest membership. As a socialist party it was, furthermore, closest ideologically to the KPD, although it did not enjoy the latter's uniquely privileged position as favourite of the occupying power. Towards the end of 1945 it became clear to the leaders of the communist party that their initial popularity with the population - assisted by their own deliberately moderate approach - would not last and that the KPD would become increasingly isolated. In free elections they could not hope to gain workable majorities over the other parties.

For these reasons, then, the KPD, assisted by the

SMAD, suddenly reversed its previous tactics and exerted pressure on the SPD for unification of both parties. The pressure took the form of verbal exhortations, prohibitions of speech, imprisonments, material inducements and even bribes of leading SPD officials, but many SPD members themselves, especially soon after the war, had already nurtured the hope that a unification would consolidate the workers' movement and give moderate socialists access to power through the KPD. Both sides, therefore, hoped for advantages. In a somewhat breathtaking re-writing of history the KPD publicly claimed that it had traditionally followed a logical policy of maintaining the unity of socialism against the fascist enemy, conveniently forgetting that it was the communists who had been largely responsible for allowing Hitler to seize power in 1933 by concentrating their hostilities against the SPD rather than the immediate Nazi threat.

At an important conference of 30 representatives each from the KPD and the SPD (the so-called "Conference of Sixty") in December 1945 the SPD expressed its dissatisfaction about the pressures being exerted on its members, complaining about the inequality of its position vis-a-vis the communists and demanding a secret ballot of its own members on the proposed unification. Subjected to massive pressure, however, the SPD leaders caved in and agreed in principle to the merger, which was specifically referred to in the joint communique after the meeting. The only permitted referendum of SPD members took place in West Berlin the following March, with 82% voting against the merger, although 62% favoured co-operation with the KPD.

The new Socialist Unity Party (SED) was finally created at Easter 1946. From its inception up till 1948 the membership rose from over 1.2 million to almost 2 million, representing 16% of the adult population of the Soviet Zone. Truly a party of the masses and of the majority of the working population, it could not be dismissed as a traditional communist party. According to its own statutes important party posts were divided equally between former SPD and KPD members (the "parity principle") and it was publicly committed, not to the Soviet model, but to a uniquely "German" and non-revolutionary path of socialism. An incidental consequence of the merger was that any links with the SPD in the Western Zone, led by the veteran Kurt Schuhmacher, were effectively cut: Schumacher had fiercely opposed the merger from the very start and was convinced that it was a flimsy pretext for a communist takeover.

The circumstances of the merger are presented quite differently in West and East German history books. In western eyes it is generally seen as a forced marriage but for official East German writers the whole process was a spontaneous union of willing partners acting in full accordance with the wishes of the grass roots membership.

3.7 The Elections of 1946

The elections in the Eastern Zone in autumn 1946 were a crucial test of the new party's appeal, as it quite openly saw itself as the leading political force (referred to as the "claim to hegemony") and faced stiff opposition from the other parties, who challenged the SED on the platforms of maintaining the unity of Germany, of preserving the pluralistic constitutional state and retaining an independant non-political civil service. The preservation of the church was also an issue kept alive by the CDU.

Although in these elections the SED did not fare badly, neither did they gain outright majorities over the other parties and they were very well aware that without their advantages in material resources and their promotion by the occupiers their performance would have been poor. To deal with the situation of potential conflict in which the SED (through the SMAD) controlled the Central Administrations but not the locally elected representative bodies of the provincial states major changes were needed and it is from this point that we can see radical moves away from party pluralism, tolerance and the "German" path to socialism.

3.8 The SED Tightens its Control

On the broader political scene worsening relations between Britain and the USA on the one hand and the Soviet Union on the other were rendering the permanent division of Germany ever more likely. When the British and American Zones were combined in 1947 the Soviets responded by setting up a powerful central organisation (the German Economic Commission) to co-ordinate the activities of the Central Administrations and direct economic planning for the Soviet Zone as a whole. The Commission was given law-making powers, was led by an SED party member and was a giant step along the road to a separate East German state under permanent Soviet control. From now on the Russians, working closely with the SED and, in particular, Walter Ulbricht, who had emerged as the leading figure in the party, promoted for the first time an intensive anti-American and anti-West German propaganda campaign. The Allied Control Council fell apart - and with it any joint administration of the former German Reich, two separate currencies were introduced in the zones and the Russians even attempted to force the western allies out of West Berlin by blockading the city.

3.9 The People's Congress

From November/December 1947 the SED, in a similar move to the setting up of the block of united parties, initiated the People's Congress Movement. This is described by the East Germans as a national initiative across boundaries of social class and party membership to unite the German people of both zones in participating in the reconstruction of the country and resisting the impending division (it was banned in the West). It is interpreted in the West, however, as a move to undermine the influence of CDU and the LDP and strengthen the SED's own claim to hegemony through a further centralist organisation under effective communist control. For, although the position of the CDU and LDP was not easy and their leaders were subjected to considerable harassment and pressure to conform to SED views (Jakob Kaiser, for instance, was summarily removed as CDU chairman on 20th December 1947 by the SMAD who also closed the party newspaper for a while) they remained a focus of opposition to Marxism.

3.10 New Parties

The SED effectively diluted the influence of the CDU and LDP by creating two brand new parties. The first of these, the DBD (<u>Demokratische</u> <u>Bauernpartei</u> <u>Deutschlands</u> - founded in April 1948), appealed to farm workers and peasants and was appointed with communist leaders. The second party, the NDPD (<u>National-Demokratische</u> <u>Partei</u> <u>Deutschlands</u>), founded in May 1948, was recruited mainly from former conservatives, army officers and Nazi Party members. Rather oddly the NDPD was permitted to campaign mildly against Marxism but strongly for the nationalist vote: behind the scenes, however, its leaders were SED-orientated and were counted on to support this party.

The People's Congress now came into its own. It had elected a 400-member People's Council (<u>Volksrat</u>) in March 1948 which was under the direct control of a committee of the SED. The Council promptly admitted the new parties to its own ranks, declared itself a representative body for the whole of Germany and set about drawing up a constitution for national government which it adopted in October of the same year. Clearly the People's Council was going to be the basis of a national parliament.

Meanwhile the Block of parties had not met very often owing to deep differences between the SED and the CDU/LDP. But in August 1948 the Block admitted not only the DBD and NDPD but also the Trade Union Federation or FDGB (<u>Freier</u> <u>Deutscher</u> <u>Gewerkschaftsbund</u>): the significance of this was that the FDGB was one of the mass organizations by now more or less controlled by the SED (it had actually formally renounced its traditional function as an independant trade union representing workers' interests as "obselete" and acknowledged its new central role as getting its members to fulfil work quotas). Other mass organisations followed suit, with the result that the SED wielded an overwhelming degree of power in the Block. The party system as such existed in name only.

3.11 The New Type of Party

The influx of Social Democrats into the newly founded SED did not in the end presage a moderate party of the masses or even progress along the much vaunted "German" path towards socialism. All this came to nothing when, from late 1947, the Soviet Union, reacting to deteriorating relations with the West and the danger of a "breakaway" Communist Party in Jugoslavia under the leadership of Tito, abruptly refused to tolerate anything but strict adherence to Moscow-style communism. This meant that the SED (as other East European communist parties) had to become a tightly organised, conformist "new type" party closely following the Soviet model as advocated by Lenin and practised by Stalin. The result: mass internal purges of moderates, the end of parity of former SPD with KPD members at the top, a strict hierarchical and centralist power structure and the introduction of a year's "probation" for candidates to party membership. Lengthy dossiers were compiled on all party members and promotions were dictated from the top in a similar manner to the Russian system of the "nomenclatura".

From now on till Stalin's death in 1953 Eastern Germany became a model of a Soviet-style state - a period referred to as the "Stalinisation of East Germany".

CHAPTER 4
FROM FOUNDATION TO THE PRESENT

In October 1949, shortly after West Germany was founded as a separate state integrated into the Western power block, the German Democratic Republic (GDR) was formally established from the former Soviet Zone of Occupation - the division of Germany was complete.

The formal basis of the GDR was the constitution and its parliament was the People's Chamber (Volkskammer) - in reality the former People's Council. The constitution itself could have done justice to a western democracy: a centralist government was envisaged but elected freely and by secret ballot according to the system of proportional representation; freedom of speech, press and religion, etc. was guaranteed, as were the rights to strike and hold private property. A special feature, however, was Article 6 which outlawed "agitation against democratic institutions" and was subsequently used by the SED to render any form of political opposition to itself a crime.

4.1 The National Front of Democratic Germany

Using a tried and tested tactic the SED in October 1949 established another kind of block of united interests, this time the National Front of Democratic Germany to which all political parties and mass organisations belonged and which was controlled by numerous secretariats that were extensions of the SED itself. The organisation of the Front extended to all regions and villages, even down to "house communities" (Hausgemeinschaften) which controlled ordinary inhabitants of a house or block of flats with no political affiliation.

The Front was probably the most sophisticated and all-pervasive device hitherto implememted by the SED. The influence of "oppositional" parties vanished, as was shown in the elections of 1950. Here candidates of all parties were presented to the electorate in a so-called "unity list" (Einheitsliste) which had been drawn up by the National Front and accepted by the old "Block" and which effectively meant that a voter could only cast his vote en bloc for a single list of candidates from all parties and not for individuals or distinct parties from that list (party affiliation was not even mentioned on the ballot paper). The SED had a built-in majority in the list and even candidates of the other parties had to be approved by them. In the national parliament, the SED were ensured 25% of seats plus 30% which were automatically allocated to the mass organisations under SED control anyhow. All key ministries were subsequently staffed by the SED, who also provided the leaders of the five provinces of the GDR. In 1952 even these vestiges of the non-centralist traditions of old Germany disappeared in favour of 14 Regions (Bezirke) which simplified the administration of the country for the SED.

This highly centralised apparatus was termed "Democratic Centralism" and the Marxist ideal of the dictatorship of the proletariat was held to have been achieved at long last. The 3rd Party Congress of July 1950 was a milestone in the development and self-confidence of the SED where it publicly and finally ditched the founding principles of 1946 and affirmed by statute the commitment to "Democratic Centralism" as befitting a "new type" party.

4.2 The Economy and the First Five Year Plan

Since 1945 the economy had suffered dramatically from the effects of war destruction and reparations. Factory plant, railway lines, and transport systems were uplifted wholesale to the Soviet Union which not only received a proportion of continuing industrial production but also further required that its own zone should make up for what was being refused from western Germany. The division of the country anyhow produced an imbalance in resources, with the east devoid of raw materials, much heavy industry or even a major port. Neither was it as rich agriculturally as is often claimed. The massive ecomonic assistance made available to West Germany through the American Marshall Plan was blocked by the Soviet Union for its new East European satellites. Naturally the standard of living of the ordinary population remained low.

The new GDR was swiftly incoporated economically into the Eastern Bloc. It became a member of the Council for Mutual Economic Assistance (an economic union of communist states, referred to in the west as COMECON or, more properly, as the CMEA) and by 1954 the new state was conducting 75% of its external trade with CMEA's members.

The economy was managed according to medium or long term "plans" determined by the SED and inherited from the Soviet model. The famous "Five Year Plan" for 1951-1955 was a typical example. Its aims were increases of almost 200% in industrial output (which would have been double that of 1936), 25% in agricultural production, 60% in the national income and 72% in work productivity. A notable improvement in living standards was promised. In the event this promise could not be fulfilled, with some basic foods remaining rationed and consumer items either unavailable or too expensive for ordinary workers. Partly this was due to a calculated and extreme concentration on heavy industrial production (e.g. steel) at the expense of consumer goods, a policy which the regime subsequently acknowledged to be mistaken.

The grafting of Soviet methods onto a historically west European industrial society was bound to create difficulties. By 1952 most important industrial activities were state-owned and organised into co-operatives (Volkseigene Betriebe or VEBs) subject to centralist control. Workers themselves had to adjust to Soviet-style exhortations to work more and to propaganda stressing the creativity of work in place of actual material incentives. Despite quite heroic achievements in the face of a reduced industrial base and an alien and impractical economic philosophy - the solution to problems lay in "reading more Lenin" or in following more strictly Stalin's pronouncements on industrialisation - the GDR remained unattractive for its inhabitants and 1.4 million people fled between 1949 and 1955 to the more prosperous and freer West Germany. The SED's relations with the professional and middle classes (who were heavily taxed and otherwise persecuted), with the church and large scale farmers were particularly bad.

In 1955 the results of the first Five Year Plan were as follows: industrial production had indeed doubled and worker productivity risen by 54% (reasonably close to the revised target of 60%). Constant price increases and shortages of consumer commodities, however, could not satisfy the expectations of a population which was bombarded with rhetoric about the achievements of socialism but in practice took conditions in the Federal Republic as the yardstick of material progress.

4.3 The "New Course" (1953)

Long before the formal conclusion of the first Five Year Plan, however, the economy had staggered into crisis with acute shortages of basic consumer goods - including food - producing widespread popular unrest by early 1953. Stalin's death in March 1953 was like the lifting of a lid from a pressure cooker of troubles and tensions. The SED had always been intensely loyal to Stalin - in many respects more Stalinist than the Soviets themselves - and the party suffered shock and internal upheaval when the line from Moscow suddenly changed to a more conciliatory attitude towards the West and tolerance of a degree of private enterprise designed to raise the standard of living. In compliance the SED agreed to compromise its all-out concentration on heavy industry, to let privately run concerns re-open, to promote contracts between business owners and the state-run distribution network (this, it was hoped, would ease the chronic supply and distribution problems which had plagued the country) and to permit landowners who had fled to the West to return in order to re-cultivate their land which had suffered neglect in the meantime. Not only price rises and taxation were eased, but pressure on the church was also relaxed.

4.4 The Uprising of 17th June 1953

Unfortunately the "New Course" came too late to prevent a workers' uprising on the 17th June 1953 and to some extent it was the attempt at liberalisation which produced the uprising itself. The external events of the 17th June are as follows:

- On the 16th June 1953 300 workers on a building site in Berlin react to a raising of work norms (i.e. a fall in wages) by spontaneously staging a protest march to the city's trade union headquarters and government ministry offices. The marchers swell rapidly in number - especially as officials refuse to see them - so that by the following day (the 17th) over 15000 workers from all of the major industries in Berlin are at a mass gathering in the Walter Ulbricht Stadium openly demanding the resignation of the government, free elections - even the re-unification of Germany.

- The Soviet City Commandant declares a state of emergency and calls in Russian troops who quickly disperse the demonstrators and impose a curfew.

- Order is restored, but the the protest spreads swiftly to other industrial centres of East Germany, where it is also put down by the Russians, often with violence (between about 20 and 300 people may have lost their lives).

Officially the East German government still blames western "agents and provocators" for planning and organising the uprising but there is little doubt that pent up economic frustration in a traditionally militant section of the workforce (the Berlin building workers) was in tune with a more widespread discontent which transformed a spontaneous action into a general political protest. The protest was over within a few days and deeply shook the

SED. It was clear that the party had become utterly remote from the workers who had been unable to settle their grievances with the Trade Union Federation (the FDGB saw itself merely as a party tool for implementing the new work norms) and who were ironically excluded from the immediate benefits of the "New Course". In the event, however, the arch-Stalinist Ulbricht survived by the skin of his teeth because Moscow feared that ditching him (they may well have had this in mind) would be seen as weakness and give courage to further opposition. Hereafter on the one hand the liberalisation policies heralded in the "New Course" were continued, while, on the other, the government periodically implemented purges, arrests and persecution of opposition elements.

4.5 The New Course Continued .... and Ended

With falls in food prices and increased availability of cars, radios, furniture, etc, things got better in the GDR. The improvement was assisted by the Soviet Union, which waived reparations from the beginning of 1953, handed over those industries over which it had retained direct control and limited the cost of stationing its troops on East German soil.

The "thaw" did not last long. At its 4th Party Conference in Spring 1954 the SED declared the "New Course" over and done with.

For one reason, it proved impossible to stem the frightening flood of refugees to the West - each year now an average of one quarter of a million. Clearly, sops to consumerism were not working on the morale of the very people the SED needed and claimed to represent, i.e. workers and the young educated.

For another, "opposition" as such was going underground since the obvious failure of the June 1954 uprising. This usually took the form of unwillingness to fulfil work quotas and similar forms of passive resistance at local level.

Not only was the "New Course", therefore, unsuccessful in achieving its aims of satisfying the population's material expectations, but Ulbricht himself, having survived the change of climate in Moscow, was able to consolidate his own position as a hard liner within the SED and purge the party of moderates. This time the purge took the form of reducing the number of elected officials in favour of younger and specially schooled functionaries directly selected by the leadership. All party members - not just officials - were personally interviewed by a commission of investigation to determine their loyalty and many of these - especially the older ones and former Social Democrats - were expelled or reduced to the status of "candidates".

4.6 Sovereignty

Despite a certain warming of relations between the Eastern and Western Blocks since the death of Stalin, no agreement could be reached on a scheme to reunite the two Germanies. Notwithstanding the rhetoric of leading politicians in both the Federal Republic and the GDR, each side was basically too distrustful of the other and had too much invested in the status quo to really desire change based on compromise (the West German leader, Konrad Adenauer, was instrumental in rejecting a plan for an independent Germany guaranteed by the allied powers which had been advanced in 1953 by Churchill). Anyhow it was the major powers, the USA and the USSR, which determined events and these had once again failed to agree on a formula for reunification at a conference of foreign ministers in Berlin in early 1954.

From 1952 East Germany had already been fortifying its border with the West and, in March 1954, it received "enlarged rights of sovereignty" from the USSR which effectively ended the formal occupation and cemented its division from the FRG. The "Two-States-Theory" - i.e. that the socialist system in the GDR could not be sacrificed for any future reunification and that the basis for unification would have to be free negotiations between the two Germanies as equal partners - was formally enunciated by both the East Germans and the Soviet leader, Khruschev. This represented a strong commitment by the USSR to a permanent East German state and the final burial of the idea of free, open-ended elections throughout Germany as a possible path towards a new united Germany.

Almost immediately, in May 1955, East Germany joined the communist military alliance, the Warsaw Pact, and became a full partner following rapid rearmament and the establishment of the National People's Army (Die Nationale Volksarmee or NVA) in 1956 (this process had in fact begun some time before in the guise of militarised police units) . The NVA is seen in the East as a "socialist coalition army", for it does not have its own general staff and is subject to the general control of the Warsaw Pact and of the USSR.

4.7 The State of the Nation in 1955

The acquisition of national sovereignty, the conclusion of the first Five Year Plan, the abandonment of the "New Course" and the end of the first decade of the post-war period are useful points at which to review the "state of the nation".

By now over 87% of gross industrial production is through the state-owned VEBs and key areas such as heavy industry, engineering and energy are almost entirely state controlled. Internal trade and business is divided equally among the state itself, private hands and co-operatives. As for agriculture, changes here have taken place more slowly, but by 1955 27% of the land is farmed by either the state itself or socialist co-operatives, with farm machinery in the hands of special stations supplying all sectors. The state has become the major providor of work in the land and initiated a revolution in employment patterns and property ownership.

For the ordinary person the standard of living is slightly improved - though rapidly falling behind that of

West Germany which is still considered as a yardstick by both the SED and the people. Price rises, shortages and deficiencies in the quality of available goods make life difficult and there is an acute housing shortage. There are signs that the SED itself is aware of the problems, which are severely compounded by an excessive, stifling bureaucracy and by inflexible over-centralisation: indeed the party discusses these internally at the highest levels but for public purposes and in the state-controlled media the message remains one of optimistic progress, of the achievements of the GDR and of the benefits of common ownership of the nation's industrial and geographical assets. Remedies to the economic misery and lack of public confidence in government are conceived in terms of even greater control and more directives ....

4.8 Destalinisation Revisited

The New Course had been officially jettisoned in the GDR in 1954, but, under pressure from the Kremlin, the SED was once again compelled to distance itself from its long established reverence for Stalin and his methods. This was part of a general process in communist countries and would have different effects in each (Albania remained "loyal" to Stalin while Hungarians felt encouraged to revolt against the communist system as a whole in 1956). The Russians themselves adopted a new, more conciliatory stance and above all accepted the principle of peaceful co-existence with non-communist countries and acknowledged that some nations might wish to follow a non-revolutionary - i.e. parliamentary - path to socialism which did not necessitate violent upheaval. All this created problems for the SED and Ulbricht who remained at heart an arch-Stalinist.

Nevertheless concessions were made. In 1956/7 the The People's Chamber passed a law which devolved some power to the local regions and allowed them to elect committees and administer government directives. Over 20000 prisoners were released, among them formerly high-ranking officials and politicians who had opposed

Ulbricht. The lot of the workers was also rendered more bearable - perhaps the party had learned the lesson of 1953 - when a house building programme was announced, a 45-hour week in the engineering industry introduced and "workers' committees" set up for a brief period to improve consultation.

4.9 Opposition and the Harich Group

Partly under the influence of events in other communist countries (the Hungarians revolted in 1956) and stimulated through limited destalinisation, intellectual opposition to Ulbricht grew at this time, especially in the universities and among young Marxists who contrasted the ideals and writings of the communist philosophers with the reality of life in the GDR. If Marx could advocate changing social reality, then why could this not be done in a so-called Marxist society?

Such views embodying the "Third Way" towards socialism (i.e. neither capitalist nor SED-Stalinist in its ideology) found a brief focus in the activities of the so-called Harich Group of 1956/7.

Wolfgang Harich was a professor of philosophy, editor and leading SED ideologist. He became the centre of a small group of highly placed intellectuals who demanded immediate de-stalinisation by such measures as personnel changes within the SED, restoration of genuine democracy (e.g. by transforming the The People's Chamber into a sovereign parliament), the ending of compulsory collectivisation, a reduction in the bureacracy, and the dissolution of the secret police. Although Harich honestly conceived such a platform as a revival of the ideal of the old "German" path towards socialism and wanted to retain the leading role of the communist party by reforming the SED from within, his ideas were perceived as especially dangerous, particularly as he tried to elicit support from West Germany and other East European countries (even the Soviet Union). The SED's reaction was swift and harsh: in 1957 Harich and half a dozen other leaders of the group were imprisoned for several years. In December of the same year "diversionary" offences, such as propaganda against the state and contacts with non-communist powers were outlawed and could be punished by prison.

4.10 Neutralisation of Opposition and the "Completion of Socialism"

Although Harich and his group had gone too far too quickly and too openly, the SED leadership was itself secretly split between the hardline Stalinist, Ulbricht, and those around the Politbureau members, Karl Schirdewan and Ernst Wollweber, who, encouraged for a while by the Soviet leader, Khrushchev, favoured a more moderate pace towards socialism. Schirdewan was "cadre" secretary of the Central Committee of the SED, responsible for personnel, while Wollweber, as Minister of State Security, controlled the secret police. Because the Hungarian uprising made the Soviet Union too nervous to encourage further experiments, however, support for Schirdewan crumbled, and Ulbricht was able to remove his opponents from power within the party. Their "revisionism" and "opportunism" were publicly condemmed.

The purges of 1958 to 1960 also involved a group of economic planners around the Minister for Heavy Industry, Fritz Selbmann, who, for a few months in 1958, formed a "managers' front" challenging the harshness of Ulbricht's policies. One member of the group, Gerhart Ziller, who was economic secretary of the Central Committee, committed suicide rather than face long imprisonment. Carve-ups in the leadership were parallelled by a large-scale clean-up in the general membership of the SED. During 1958 and 1959 about 60,000 were expelled, many district leaders where removed from office and approximately 300,000 were "re-selected" after having been found reliable after examination.

Ulbricht's personal position in the party was at this point stronger than ever and he would remain First

Secretary of the Central Committee until 1971. His leadership and policies were confirmed at the 5th Party Congress in July 1958, which also laid the foundations for a new economic plan and the "completion" of the process of socialist reconstruction. It was here that Ulbricht uttered the famous - and in the light of experience unfortunate - claim that by 1961 the GDR would have caught up with the FRG in consumer living standards.

One year into the second Five Year Plan the economic situation in the GDR had indeed improved significantly. By 1959 industrial production had jumped by 12% for two years running and food ration cards for meat, butter and sugar had disappeared. Basic foodstuffs were subsidisd and a workers' social welfare system encompassing hospitals, rest homes and holidays was well appreciated. In 1958 even the number of citizens leaving the country dropped.

These improvements and the consolidation of the leadership had prompted the SED to overreach itself and embark on an over-ambitious and unrealistic programme of economic recovery designed to catch up with and overhaul West Germany. Early in 1958 the administrative apparatus for the nation's economy was prepared, with the State Planning Commission (Staatliche Plankommission) either taking over or co-ordinating the functions of previous ministries. Trade Unions acquired more responsibility for the social welfare of their workers and efforts were made to co-ordinate the activities of local administrative units as well as affording them more power. In October 1958 the previous Five Year Plan - which had only been in force for two years - was officially scrapped and the new Seven Year Plan launched with its "main economic target" of matching the Federal Republic and demonstrating once and for all the superiority of the socialist system.

In detail the plan - which ran in tandem with a similar plan for the USSR and its allies - envisaged an increase in work productivity of 85% and major growth in the chemical and electrical industries. The production of consumer goods such as motor cars, televisions, washing machines and refrigerators would increase significantly, as would agricultural goods and foreign trade turnover.

Although some targets were nearly achieved and the GDR established itself as the second largest industrial nation in the Eastern Block after the Soviet Union, the goals were grandiose and had to be quietly revised in 1962 along more modest and realistic lines: in particular the projected 5.8% annual economic growth rate was abandoned in the light of an overall increase of just 3%.

On the broad political front the influence of the traditional "oppositional" parties as such had by now virtually vanished and these even faced rapidly declining membership rolls.

4.11 Collectivisation of Agriculture

One of the prime target areas for the "completion of socialism" in the GDR remained in 1957 the organisation of agricultural production and its removal from private hands into co-operatives (Landwirtschaftliche Produktionsgenossenschaften or LPGs). This process had been progressing slowly since 1952 but was dramatically accelerated between 1957 - when just 25% of farming land was under LPG control - and 1960, when LPGs managed almost 85% of the land and had all but eliminated the independant farmer. Officially the farmers willingly joined the LPGs, but in truth threats and coercion - even imprisonment - were measures liberally applied in the face of often stubborn resistance after prolonged haranguing had failed. A major initiative involved the transformation of Type I LPGs, in which the co-operative owned only the arable land and the farmer retained his pasture land and animal stock, into LPGs Type III, where all three categories belonged to the collective.

Small trades and crafts were another area which had escaped large scale collectivisation, but, again, between 1958 and 1960, they were incorporated into appropriate co-operatives - though still not quite so extensively as the farmers.

4.12 The State Council (Staatsrat) and Increased Unpopularity of the SED

In the political arena, 1960 saw the abolition of the post of President (held by the veteran Wilhelm Pieck until his death in the same year) and the creation of a powerful new organ, the State Council (Staatsrat), whose chairman - not surprisingly - was Walter Ulbricht. Elected by the People's Council for four years it called national elections, was able to call referenda, concluded international treaties, appointed and approved ambassadors and interpreted and implemented laws as well as making some of its own.

Ulbricht was by now the focus of an unprecedented concentration of individual power and of an official personality cult which was in inverse proportion to his actual popularity with the ordinary populace.

Further unpopular measures by the state included the official suspension of the legal right to strike and an increase in the powers of the Conflict Commissions (Konfliktkommissionen) at places of work entitling them to dispense minor punishments. Such measures were bound to be perceived as an erosion of traditional rights and as a travesty of justice under a socialist government more concerned with the fulfilment of production quotas than workers' welfare.

4.13 The Crisis of 1961 and the Berlin Wall

The enforced and hasty collectivisation of land was an economic disaster in the immediate term. The new LPGs neglected a lot of their new land and shortages in meat and dairy products ensued. Even the rate of increase in industrial production dropped sharply between 1959 and 1961 as a result of the new economic and planning measures. The difficulties of the ambitious Seven Year

Plan were further aggravated by strikes and by the West Germans' cancellation of the inter-German trade treaty in 1960. This action had been prompted by the East Germans' insistence that West German citizens required special passes to enter the Eastern Sector of Berlin: admittedly West Germany restored the treaty just two months later, but it demonstrated to the GDR the dangers of economic dependance on the West. The status of West Berlin had in fact been a long-standing bone of contention, with the USSR exerting great pressure on the Western Allies to withdraw. Its main problem from the East German point of view was that it provided an easy escape route to the West for its dissatisfied citizens. Officially the government of the GDR blamed, not its own policies, but the escapees for the rapidly deteriorating economic situation, and there is little doubt that a mass exodus of its workforce threatened, by July 1961, to cripple the economy at a rate from which it could not recover. The GDR leadership had reacted by appointing veteran Stalinists, Alfred Neumann and Karl Mewis, to key positions in economic planning. They reinforced the uncompromising approach. A vitriolic propaganda campaign against the West and draconian punishments for refugees who were caught merely fuelled the furnace of discontent.

The crunch came in the summer of 1961 when the USSR made renewed threats over West Berlin and many East German citizens felt that the bolt hole to the West would shortly be closed: in July an unprecedented 30000 swarmed into the western sector of the city, in August 47000. Although the Russians stopped short of applying further military pressure on West Berlin (e.g. by severing both land and air links), they decided to cut off the western sector completely by erecting a wall down the centre of the city: this was begun in the night of the 12th August 1961 and effectively made the populace of the GDR prisoners of their own country. The "Wall" itself promptly became a potent symbol of the division of Germany and, for West Germans, a stark embodiment of the repression of their compatriots and of the political, economic and moral bankruptcy of communism.

From the end of the war until the building of the Berlin Wall over three million people had used Berlin to escape from the East, most of them to West Germany. A peak of almost one third of a million East Germans had left in the crisis year of 1953 and there were seldom fewer than two hundred thousand refugees every year. In particular doctors (among numerous professional people), young citizens and trained industrial workers figured prominently in the exodus.

4.14 After the Wall

The immediate period after the building of the Berlin Wall was a difficult and frightening time for many East German citizens. Official pamphlets publicly incited young people and workers to beat up and abuse "enemies" and "provocators", i.e. individuals who had expressed opposition to SED policies or even whose attendance at work had been poor. On the 20th September 1961 Ulbricht and the State Council gave themselves unlimited powers for a state of emergency which could be called in time of war or peace. Although this darkness lasted only a few months till the end of the year, the climate of violence and fear and the awesome power of the party were strongly reminiscent of the hysterical and dangerous atmosphere of the Nazi period.

The SED was all set for a renewed rehabilitation of Stalinism - the brand of communism it had always felt at home with - and was therefore completely wrong-footed and taken aback when Moscow abruptly initiated a new phase of liberalism and de-stalinisation at the 22nd Conference of the Communist Party of the Soviet Union. It was at this conference that the Soviet CP proclaimed its goals of matching the industrial production of the USA by 1970 and of creating consumer surpluses for all (including free use of all public services such as transport, gas and electricity, free meals in restaurants and a 35-hour working week) by 1980. Although there is little evidence that the population of either the Soviet Union or the GDR took such unrealistic promises at all seriously (they were never fulfilled), they did represent the start of a new effort on the part of communist governments to "sell" socialism by both ideological persuasion and increases in economic productivity. Ulbricht was very much a part of this new drive and - as always - followed the Moscow line faithfully. The closing of the West Berlin escape hatch also stabilised the GDR internally: the massive haemorrhage of its workforce ceased and individuals also adjusted to making the best of opportunities in the country as it stood.

The 6th Party Conference of the now one and a half million strong SED in January 1963 was the next landmark in the evolution of the GDR. It was quite an international affair, with the Soviet leader (Khruschev) present, and representatives from the entire communist world, including China, which was very soon (1963) to split away from the Moscow-led international movement and commit itself to a much more militant, dogmatic and revolutionary approach. As for the GDR itself, however, the conference was a prestige event at which the East Germans reaffirmed the leading role of the Soviet Union.

4.15 The New Economic System (1963) and the Age of Socialism

In the reshuffle of the top party apparatus which took place at the 6th Conference, new and younger faces appeared on the Central Committee, heralding a new and more professional approach to the crisis in - the still falling - industrial output. One of these was the economist and engineer Erich Apel, who initiated a thoroughgoing reform and fundamental change in the direction of the economic system. The reform, the so-called "New Economic System", was initiated at the conference and formally launched in June 1963. Its basis was a strengthening of the "material interest" of the worker in productivity instead of mere ideological and moral exhortation, i.e. an element of capitalist-type incentive and reward would be introduced. In detail the new scheme envisaged the central planning authority (the State

Planning Commission) working out five to seven year plans in consultation with the 82 umbrella organisations for factories (VVBs = Vereinigungen Volkseigener Betriebe). The factories themselves were given more independance in buying in materials and arranging credit, as well as in structuring prices, wages and incentive schemes. The New Economic System (NES) dominated the First Party Programme of the SED, which was adopted at the 1963 Party Congress. This programme summarised the fundamental political positions of the party, reviewing German history since the First World War (1914-1918) and giving the party's interpretation of developments in East and West Germany since 1945. According to the programme the "Age of Socialism" had now begun in the GDR.

In parallel with the NES a move was initiated to re-organise the SED along the lines of the "production principle", according to which party units corresponded to activities in building, industry and agriculture. This party structure would reflect economic organisation and would be most appropriate to a workers' party. The complete changeover to the production principle was abandoned in 1966 in favour of the older "territorial principle", however, when too many technologically and professionally minded younger members were threatening the dominance of the the older guard at the middle level, but it did leave an enduring impression on the character of the SED. Both the rise and fall of the adoption of the production principle had in fact followed closely similar developments in the Soviet Union under Khruschev, who had started it all and who retired from the political arena in 1966.

4.16 The Constitution of 1968

In 1967 and 1968 the SED initiated important changes in the penal code and the state constitution which represented even greater consolidation of the socialist state and further moves away from the traditional institutions of the old unified Germany. The persistent and fundamental insecurity of the SED was demonstrated not least by the draconian punishments - long prison sentences and even the death penalty - prescribed for political offences. The new "socialist" constitution of 1968 was approved by people's referendum and is notable in its very first article for officially endowing the SED with the role of leading party in the land: in other words, any dispute of this role became an offence against the legal constitution of the state. Actually this represented merely the final and open statement of a long-standing reality that was also reflected in Article 2, which embodied "socialist ownership of the means of production, planning and management of social development. Elsewhere, although the document superficially resembled western type constitutions through its investment of ultimate power in the parliamentary body (The People's Chamber) and through the guarantees of freedom of person, press, radio, media and of religious belief, such formulae merely obscured the de facto controlling position of the SED and did not in themselves indicate at all how such freedoms were defined in practice. The constitutional guarantee of free elections by secret ballot was also quite worthless since most elections had long been conducted in blatant violation of the rule of secrecy as public celebrations of mass support for the SED.

4.17 The Prague Spring of 1968

In the same year as the new constitution was adopted, East German soldiers joined with Soviet and other Eastern Block troops in marching into Czechoslovakia to displace the liberal socialist administration under Alexander Dubcek, which had found broad support from the people in attempting to move away from the rigidly centralised Soviet model towards greater individual freedoms and genuinely democratic institutions. By participating in the swift crushing of the "Prague Spring" of 1968 the GDR cemented its position as a trusted military partner of the Soviet Union and confirmed itself as solidly inside the dictatorial-bureacratic mould of post-Stalin communism which would not tolerate sudden programmes of liberalisation and democratisation.

4.18   A New Confidence: the Science of Socialism?

Towards the end of the 1960s, perhaps in the wake of the success of the New Economic System and in view of the unassailable position of the SED together with its close relationship with the USSR, Walter Ulbricht entered a philosophical phase in which he began to enlarge the ideological concept of socialism on the basis of the East German experience. In a nutshell, he suggested that the GDR had been the first highly industrialised country in the world to convert itself entirely to the socialist system - moreover under the most difficult conditions of post-war recovery and national dismemberment - and prove its success.

The implications of this claim were far-reaching. For one thing it constituted something of a revision of the Marxist theory that socialism was just a transitory phase on the road to a truly communist society in which the economic - and capitalist-derived - categories of money, property, profit and financial incentive would completely disappear. Ulbricht claimed that socialism was in fact much more than a rather unutopian "middle phase", that it had semi-permanent systematic character and values of its own, and, in particular, that its application in the GDR demonstrated clearly that the old economic categories need not be regarded as wholly negative or even as inherent to capitalism. Furthermore the "system character" of socialism was held to be scientific in its very nature, so that proper and thorough analysis of its laws could be used as the basis to govern successfully all human activities. These ideas now led to a burst of "scientific" Marxist-Leninist ideology applied to all sciences, arts and professional fields, with the result that a new breed of highly educated functionaries schooled in the theory of socialism emerged alongside the old party veterans. Machinery was also set up to conduct sophisticated analysis of public opinion and apply techniques of propaganda and manipulation in order to bridge the gap between party and people more effectively.

The second important consequence of Ulbricht's notions

on scientific socialism was that the GDR began to see itself as being a model for the communist world, which represented a clear challenge to Soviet hegemony.

As if to reinforce and embody the ideological claims, Ulbricht himself, holding all positions of power in the apparatus of party and state, had become very much a cult figure in the official eye of the GDR and was feted beyond all reason.

Despite such apparent confidence all was not well with the East German economy or with the political future of Walter Ulbricht. It was true that heavy industrial production had risen considerably and that the supply of many luxury consumer goods (motor cars, washing machines and television sets, etc) had reached a peak around 1966/67. Even agriculture had begun gradually to recover from the shock of enforced and over-hasty collectivisation. The problem was that the gap with the more prosperous Federal Republic had started to widen again and the stated aim of parity associated with the last Five Year Plan was not going to be achieved. Indeed, in the energy sector and the supply and building industries the shortfall from the planned targets was considerable. All this was aggravated by an acute labour shortage which was claimed to be the worst of any industrial country and was partly still a legacy of the pre-Berlin Wall exodus. In addition the GDR was failing in its trade commitments to the Soviet Union. In 1970, therefore, the party, under Ulbricht, contemplated a radical return to strategies of economic centralisation in order to reverse the decline. The old pattern of oscillation between reform and retrenchment was about to repeat itself. In fact, Ulbricht's demise was very near, although one further factor which contributed to his downfall should be considered in more detail: viz. that of the changing relations with the Federal Republic.

4.19 Relations with the Federal Republic: The Long Road to Ostpolitik

To understand the significance of the state of relations between East and West Germany, a brief review of the issue is helpful at this point.

It may be recalled that the paper resolution of the Allies' to treat Germany as a unity immediately after the war was never fulfilled and that, with partitioning and the establishment of two sovereign states, there was scant prospect of re-unification.

4.20 Stalin's Note of 1952

In 1952, however, Stalin sent a note to the Western powers in which he proposed setting up a united German state with whom the Allies would then conclude a proper "Peace Treaty" which in turn would set up the conditions for restoring Germany to the family of independant nations. The Russians also declared themselves willing to allow free elections throughout Germany, although they insisted that the Allies, and not the United Nations, should supervise such elections. Stalin's note was not taken seriously by the West, which was busy integrating the Federal Republic into its own power bloc, and no such chance presented itself again. Quite possibly Stalin intended no more than to delay this integration or even detach the Federal Republic from the western camp with the prospect of re-unification - an ideal which appealed to most Germans on both sides of the border. It is also unlikely that the Russians had the same concept of free elections as the West and would have adopted previous tactics in attempting to stifle the participation of non-communist parties. Whatever the genuineness of Stalin's famous note, it is certain that the SED, who supported these proposals with the slogan, "Germans around the same table", would have rapidly disappeared in a united Germany conducting truly free elections, but the rejection of Stalin's proposals set the stage for the petrification of the status quo for many years and for both East and West German governments to indulge in much public posturing of their commitment to the emotive issue of re-unification without having to do anything about it (e.g. compromise). For a brief period, however, the SED was genuinely afraid that the USSR was considering selling the German communist party down the river in return for a neutral united Germany.

4.21 The Long Freeze and the "Two States" Theory

After Stalin's death in 1953 there was renewed interest between the Western powers and the USSR on the reunification issue, but the differences could not be resolved. The West now insisted that free elections throughout the two Germanies should take place before any moves towards unification and - supported by the West German Chancellor, Adenauer - wanted Germany to be able to participate in a western military alliance. The Russians, however, saw a provisional pan-German administration as the preliminary step to elections and could not tolerate the possibility of a non-neutral German state incorporated into the western bloc (Foreign Ministers' Conference in Berlin 1954). Finally, in 1955, in East Berlin, the Soviet leader, Khrushchev, formulated the "Two States Theory", by which the USSR finally committed itself to the long-term reality of two separate Germanies: the implications of this statement were that Russia would not sacrifice the GDR and its political structures in any future deal over unification, and that negotiations for unity would have to proceed from contacts and discussions between the two Germanies as equal partners. The Russians were now fully committed to the GDR - which received sovereignty and was relieved of its status as an occupied country -, especially as West Germany was being rapidly re-armed as a military partner of the USA and Britain.

The Russian move undoubtedly marked the point of no return in the question of re-unification. The basic difference remained that of a West Germany demanding free elections as a precursor to unification and of the East

Germans insisting first on a provisional government: according to a proposal by Ulbricht in 1957 - which was again rejected by the West Germans -, this provisional government could take the form of a German Council consisting of an equal number of representatives from each country who would constitute a kind of confederation. Adenauer, on the other hand, felt that a "position of strength" and aggressive no compromise on elections was the best stance to adopt because it would force a climbdown on the part of the East Germans and the Russians, but it is now clear that, although this approach had popular appeal at the time, it had little chance of achieving any real progress. Proposals from the East Germans, like those for a confederation, or, as in 1960, Ulbricht's suggestion for a treaty to renounce the use of force and guarantee mutual non-intervention, were perceived entirely by Bonn as efforts to gain formal recognition as a state. West Germany, of course, had refused outright to acknowledge the GDR as a sovereign nation and - through the so-called Hallstein Doctrine - indeed threatened to break off diplomatic relations with any third country which itself recognised East Germany. The very constitution of the FRG was regarded in the West as provisional until such time as the Germans in the East were in a position to exercise true self-determination, pending which their only "representatives" were the West Germans themselves (the so-called "sole right of representation"). Evidently relations between the two Germanies were being deliberately maintained at a level of permanent hostility. The East Germans re-iterated their proposals for a confederation leading to re-unification in the "National Document" of 1962, secure in the knowledge that they would never be taken up in West Germany, which refused to conduct any talks.

Some small movement did take place when, at Christmas 1963, the two sides negotiated an agreement which allowed, for the first time in two and a half years, West Berliners to visit relatives in the Eastern sector of the city. From November 1964 old age pensioners in the GDR were allowed out to visit relatives in the West (being "unproductive" their defection would not have troubled the authorities). However, in the same year, a letter by Ulbricht to the new West German leader, Chancellor Erhard, resurrecting the idea of a joint "German Council" with the aim of re-unification, was returned unopened. Between 1963 and 1966 various agreements enabled West Berliners to visit East Berlin, but the insistence of the West Berlin Senate that these agreements did not have political character or imply official recognition of the GDR finally led the East Germans to discontinue them.

4.22 The Open Letter of 1966

In 1966 the SED sent the West German SPD an "Open Letter" suggesting co-operation and talks on re-unification. Now this was nothing at all new and the East Germans expected the usual snub. To the astonishment of the SED, however, this time the SPD replied. Although the reply itself was highly critical of the SED and firmly ruled out the possibility of any joint declarations, it did propose further consultations. After a number of joint meetings to prepare the ground, the SED took fright and withdrew on a pretext. To some extent the party was also concerned that an open discussion on the German issue would undermine its own position vis-a-vis the population of the GDR and endanger the internal stability which had been achieved since the erection of the Berlin Wall in 1961.

When, moreover, at the end of 1966 a new government in Bonn (a coalition of the CDU under Georg Kiesinger and the SPD led by Willy Brandt) adopted at long last a more conciliatory tone to the East, the SED found itself in a quandary. The ball was suddenly in its own court.

An immediate reaction was to play down the "pan-German" feeling in East Germany by a fierce anti-West German propaganda campaign involving the deletion of the word "Germany" in all official references to

West German political parties and the highlighting of the impossibility of unification in the light of the FRG's "medieval" political conditions and rampant neo-Nazism. Early in 1967 the People's Council passed a law defining East German citizenship, which was intended to emphasize further the unique identity of the GDR. Conflict, too, arose with the Evangelical Church which had always strongly identified itself with the goal of unification.

Despite its conviction that Bonn was attempting to undermine the SED, the party undertook new initiatives in 1967. Ulbricht stated publicly that the Federal Republic would need to undergo deep social changes before the long process of reunification could be achieved but that a modus vivendi should be an immediate goal. In May 1967 Willi Stoph, Chairman of the Council of Ministers, wrote to Federal Chancellor Kiesinger proposing direct negotiations on the normalisation of relations and on the recognition of existing frontiers (as well as on the prohibition of atomic weapons and arms reductions). The letter was accepted in Bonn but achieved little: Kiesinger, by replying with suggestions for talks about co-operation on cultural and economic matters, went some way towards acknowledging the diplomatic existence of the GDR but ignored the key issue of recognition. In March of the following year Ulbricht broke off negotiations. The 7th Party Congress in 1967 made no mention of the unification question and Ulbricht was proclaiming his philosophy of the "socialist human community". Once again the SED was able to steer clear of the dangerous waters of rapprochement and retreat into internal consolidation.

4.23 Willy Brandt's Ostpolitik

Real movement came in 1969 with the new coalition of the Social Democratic and Liberal Parties in Bonn under Chancellor Brandt who declared that peace could not be achieved without the involvement of the GDR. In view of this tacit acknowledgement of East Germany's status and Brandt's overtures of detente towards the East (the so-called "Ostpolitik"), the SED's original quandary became acute. It reacted by going for gold in demanding complete formal recognition of the GDR as a foreign power and acknowledgement of the inviolability of existing borders as a precondition for talks on normal relations: West Berlin would also be regarded as politically separate from the West (Ulbricht's letter to the West German President Heinemann of the 18th December 1969). Ulbricht's hard line and personal resistance to constructive negotiations was not supported by Moscow or other communist countries at this stage, who did not go along with the traditional SED-picture of West Germany as little more than a revanchist power seeking to take over the GDR (in significant international moves the FRG concluded treaties with the USSR and Poland in December 1970).

Historic meetings between Stoph and Brandt took place in Erfurt (GDR) in March 1970 and in Kassel (FRG) the following May. Rather to the dismay of the SED Brandt's reception by the people in Erfurt was positively tumultuous.

Ulbricht's position became incompatible with Moscow's policy of international detente when he presumably attempted to sabotage the negotiations of the Four Allied Powers on the status of Berlin (in a show of strength the East German authorities subjected the traffic to and from West Berlin to renewed harassment at this point). This and further internal economic problems contributed to his sudden resignation as Party Leader and First Secretary of the Central Committee in May 1971.

4.24 Treaties

The Four Power Berlin Agreement came into force on the 3rd June 1972. It was confirmed that West Berlin was not a constitutive part of the Federal Republic to be governed therefrom. On the other hand the Federal Republic would be the consular representatives of the citizens of West Berlin abroad and through specific reference could include these in treaties and agreements.

In any respects the status issue remained unsettled and the powers retained their rights over the city. However, this accord paved the way for the Transit Agreement between East and West Germany (17.12.1971) which greatly eased traffic movement between West Berlin and the Federal Republic; travel from West Berlin into East Berlin and the GDR became much easier, too. The new East German leader, Erich Honecker, heralded in April 1972 the possibility of "normal relations" between the two countries and in the same year a Treaty on Traffic and Communications (Verkehrsvertrag) - the first between the two nations - was signed.

The culmination of the Ostpolitik was the so-called Basic Treaty (Grundlagenvertrag) of December 1972, which was designed to regulate the basis of relations between the two Germanies. Through the treaty the FRG and the GDR acknowledged each other's sovereignty and frontiers and foreswore both the use and the threat of war against one another. Mutual independance was to be respected and neither country would intervene in the other's internal and external affairs. Although the acknowledgment of national sovereignty was a partial victory for the GDR, West Germany stopped short of according the GDR full recognition as a normal foreign state by specifying (within the treaty itself) that the agreement did not affect its own long-standing commitment to the re-unification of the German people through free self-determination and that questions of nationality were not settled by the treaty.

The Basic Treaty represented a compromise of highly divergent approaches which subsequently enabled agreements to be reached on many areas of practical co-operation, e.g. trade, communications, science, culture and medical provision for visitors. The basic differences between the political and social systems remained as fundamental as before, and hopes of a major breakthrough on re-unification are probably as remote up to this day as ever they were.

For the GDR, the lifting of the Western embargo on

its international recognition led to the admittance of both Germanies to the United Nations (18th September 1973) and in particular enabled East Germany to take up diplomatic relations with many more countries than hitherto, including, in 1974, the USA.

The GDR participated in the international Conference on Security and Co-operation in Europe (meeting from 1973), of which the resulting agreements were signed by heads of state - including Erich Honecker - at the Summit Conference in Helsinki (1975). The Helsinki agreement guaranteed not only international territoral integrity and non-intervention in the affairs of member states, regardless of political system, but also incorporated a famous commitment to human rights and basic freedoms; international co-operation was also to be promoted. East and West have tended to stress different aspects of the same package of agreements, with socialist countries emphasising the legitimisation of current state boundaries and of the territorial status quo, while western nations see the issue of human freedoms as crucial. The human rights question as embodied in the Helsinki agreement has caught countries like the Soviet Union and the GDR by surprise in recent times and they have had no little internal difficulty over it. At a conference in June 1976 of 29 European socialist parties many Eurocommunist leaders explained that such concepts as the dictatorship of the proletariat, as realised in Eastern Bloc states, where genuinely free elections, a parliamentary opposition or fundamental human rights are disallowed, are no longer acceptable to the truly international socialist movement.

The dramatic breakthrough of 1969-1971 has not led to anything like complete normalisation between the two Germanies. The East Germans have adhered to a policy of "demarcation" (Abgrenzung) and many West Germans feel that the GDR is profiting handsomely from the treaties while their own state has effectively renounced all claim to lands in the east.[3] There has also been a general deterioration of western relations with the Soviet Union and a regression to a fluctuating pattern of conflict and co-operation.

4.25 From Ulbricht to Honecker

Ulbricht resigned unexpectedly as First Secretary of the Central Committee in May 1971 - obstensibly for reasons of age but almost certainly because of the country's economic problems, his recent ideological divergence from Soviet Marxism and his resistance to international detente. He was given the meaningless and powerless office of "Chairman of the SED" (the position had not existed before and disappeared with him) and he died shortly afterwards in 1973. Despite his swift fall and subsequent "erasure" Ulbricht was undoubtedly the prime architect of the present-day SED.

Any attempts to pursue policies or ideas which did not correspond exactly to those approved by the Soviet Union were now firmly ruled out and the GDR returned once more to the role of junior to the USSR. Thus, Ulbricht's final ideological "abberations" and his claims that the GDR represented a "developed social system", a "socialist human community", in which the phase of socialism acquired quasi-permanent status (and by implication a degree of ideological independance from the USSR) were now formally rejected. In the eyes of his (subsequent) critics, Ulbricht had obscured the true class differences which still persisted - despite the leading role of the proletariat - and which remained to be overcome in order for the final stage of communism to be attained. The true term for the current status quo was proclaimed to be a "developed socialist society" which was still in the process of evolving towards communism in common with the Soviet Union and other socialist states. In 1973 ideology was declared to be the "main activity" of the party ("Hauptinhalt der Tätigkeit unserer Partei"[4]) and there followed a major educational and propaganda intitiative to increase political awareness of Marxism-Leninism and commitment to the SED's aims.

Ulbricht's successor was Erich Honecker, who had risen to the top of the SED through the youth organisation, FDJ. From the very beginning, at the 8th Party Conference in June 1971, Honecker imposed a different style of national management. In place of Ulbricht's grandiose plans Honecker announced much more realistic and sober targets. First and foremost the drive for productivity and growth was to be intensified, but through industrial rationalisation and the application of modern techniques to replace old-fashioned methods. And, secondly, there took place a conscious attempt to improve the lot of the ordinary citizen through positive social policy.

4.26 Changes in Apparatus and Constitution

In 1972 the People's Chamber widened the role and powers of the Council of Ministers (Ministerrat) at the expense of those of the Council of State (Staatsrat) to include not just economic and cultural policy, but also responsibility for the implementation of home and foreign policy. With this measure the Council of Ministers effectively took over the executive power of the State Council (which was still chaired by Ulbricht who was thus further enfeebled).

In October 1974 the constitution was once again altered in order to accommodate the new realities of the post-Ulbricht period. For one thing all references to the German nation and to re-unification were eradicated. This served to remove all question of future re-unification with the West in the minds of the citizens and to emphasise the national identity of the GDR (many national institutions had been renamed in this vein, e.g. the national radio station Deutschlandsender had become Radio DDR). Furthermore the bond with the Soviet Union was stressed as being "eternal and irrevocable", while the new powers of the Council of Ministers were officially written into the constitution. As before, the leading role of the working class and "its Marxist-Leninist Party" (i.e. the SED) was enshrined in the first article.

The party apparatus and its control over all aspects of life in the GDR remained as strict as ever - indeed, it was rendered more effective through greater sophistication than had been usual in the cruder era of Ulbricht. Whereas Ulbricht had brought into the top of the party technocrats and expert economists, Honecker replaced these with young career politicians well versed in ideology and party organisation who could be expected to enhance the SED's political hegemony and halt the "slippage" from othodoxy which had marked Ulbricht's final years. Results of the return to othodoxy were seen in the strengthening of the "cadre" system and more intensified dissemination of the SED's policies throughout the general population under the watchword of "participation".

4.27 Economic Upswing and a New Social Policy

Although Honecker specifically disavowed the old planning by rhetoric and prepared the country for longer term and more realistic economic targets, the traditional policy of increasing the state controlled sector through VEBs continued, so that these accounted for 82% of industrial production in 1971 and for over 99% the following year. Despite a pesistent shortage of labour, 86% of women at work and a high percentage of the population ineligible to work through age (58% in 1973), the standard of living rose during the 1970's and was well established as the highest in the communist world: at the same time the western world was being hit by the oil crisis and entering its slide into mass unemployment. The crisis of Ulbricht's legacy 1969/70 was overcome with a decisive swing to more centralist techniques of planning and control - this time, however, with the emphasis on intensivisation and rationalisation of productivity and the avoidance of over capacity through poor co-ordination and inefficiency. In the propaganda this is often linked to the "technical-scientific revolution" achieved by the scientific application of socialist ideology in the workaday world.

From 1971 the SED announced a new programme of social improvements as part of the new "unity of economic and social policy". Not only would over a million and a quarter new homes be built or modernised by 1980 (housing had been grossly neglected under Ulbricht) but pensions, social benefit payments and wages would be increased and working mothers would also be assisted. Enhanced provision for pre-school and nursery children was further introduced at the expense of the hitherto intensive promotion of university and higher education. Changes in the provision for very young children and the youth movements were also linked to the ideological drive for a greater identification of the population with the aims and policies of the SED.

The SED's 9th Party Congress in 1976 was firmly in keeping with the new tone of the previous five years. It was a fairly sober, low-key affair, with Honecker given the new title of General Secretary of the party and confirmed in his leadership. The new economic and social direction was further underlined and a policy programme declared which remained valid into the 1980's. This programme stressed the seniority of the USSR, the leading role of the SED, the commitment to improving social conditions for the most needy and the rationalisation of industrial productivity. Honecker reported that, by the end of the previous 5-Year period, the annual national income growth rate had surpassed the planned targets (5.4% as against 4.9%) and overall industrial output had exceeded the target by 14.5 billion Marks, with a marked increase in labour productivity. Agricultural output was up by 11.1% over 1966-1970, with needs for basic foodstuffs for domestic consumption being met from home production except for sugar, fruit, vegetable and some grain products (quite a large exception, one may think). In the area of foreign policy, the programme reflected the advances made in East-West German relations, with no further mention of re-unification and the accent on the established and enduring "socialist nation" of the GDR "co-existing" with the Federal Republic and the western world.

Projected targets for the new Plan 1976-1980 included increases in labour productivity (30%), agricultural production ((20%), national investment and the promotion of basic research in science and technology: exports to socialist countries would be up by 50%. Industrial output would rise by 6% annually but great stress was laid on reduction in energy consumption - "a much more sparing use of materials is a demand of our daily work"[5] During the actual proceedings of the 9th Party Congress no mention was made of the implementation of previously planned and eagerly awaited social improvements (such as the 40 hour week, longer holidays and higher pensions). These were, however, introduced shortly after the congress in the light of widespread popular disappointment, and it may be assumed that the party leadership had gambled on postponing the measures until after the goals of increased productivity had been realised if public reaction had not been unfavourable.

4.28 Coping with Mounting Opposition and Economic Stagnation

By the mid-1970's Honecker's personal power in the GDR had increased to equal that of his predecessor, Ulbricht. As well as becoming General Secretary of the party itself in 1976, he was made Chairman of the State Council and confirmed as Chairman of the National Defence Council later the same year. Another leading figure was Willi Stoph, Chairman of the Council of Ministers.

At this moment and in the light of a split in the world communist movement the SED intensified its propaganda offensive to capture the hearts and minds of the population. The Helsinki agreements on human rights, the rejection by independant Eurocommunist parties of Stalin-type dictatorships and the movements by the Jugoslavian and Rumanian governments in a similar direction all contributed to a wave of increased opposition to the bureaucratic party hegemony, largely expressed by intellectuals, artists and writers within the GDR itself. The number of applications for exit visas from citizens wishing to leave the country increased dramatically. The details and representatives of this widespread cultural dissent are described in detail elsewhere in his book but its effects were far-reaching and taken very seriously by the SED: the "transmission" function of the mass organisations and the other parties was highlighted with the non-communist parties and the FDGB all holding congresses in 1977 to endorse the leading role of the SED. Relations with the church were, however, subjected to some strain when the Evangelical Church expressed concern at the extent to which the primacy of Marxist-Leninist ideology - as had emerged at the 9th Party Congress - appeared to endanger the future relations between church and state. Further contention arose over the introduction of "defence studies" in schools (September 1978), which the church saw as incitement to hatred and as incompatible with Christianity, although the state - generally supporting the church's initiatives on peace as long as these were directed towards the west - has been prepared to accompany censorship with flexibility. However, the determination of the SED not to tolerate dissent was evidenced in 1979 when the penal code was further strengthened. and the distribution of written materials (e.g. critical publications in West Germany) deemed hostile to the GDR became a punishable offence.

With regard to the economic improvement from 1971, the increases in industrial growth and national income slowed considerably towards the end of the decade, reflecting international energy prices (the Soviet Union, on whom the GDR is totally dependant for the supply of basic raw materials, reluctantly increased the cost of these in the light of the world demand) and the price of military aid to the third world. The slogan "intensification of production" - i.e. the most efficient use of all available resources combined with appeals to the population to maintain productivity - characterised this period and reflected economic pressures. The persistent problem in the public perception of lack of parity with the Federal Republic in terms of general living standards and anything but very basic food and goods continued to bedevil the SED, and it was exacerbated as the number of visitors from West Germany increased in the wake of the treaties of the early 1970s. Despite efforts to modernise, the GDR, by comparison with the West, still suffered time honoured problems in the production, supply and quality of consumer goods. Whether such difficulties outweigh the issues of chronic unemployment and social disruption in many western countries, however, is another question.

4.29 Relations with the West in the Early 1980s

In December 1979 the Soviet Union invaded Afghanistan, provoking a sharp deterioration in East-West relations. The deterioration was accelerated by the emergence - and suppression - of the oppositional "Solidarity" movement in Poland in 1980, which led to the Federal German leader, Helmut Schmidt, cancelling an official visit to that country. It was also clear that the GDR was so concerned at the large numbers of visitors from West Germany that it was prepared to compromise the recent inter-German agreements by unilaterally doubling the compulsory foreign exchange fee for entry in October 1980. Honecker even went so far as to renew demands for full diplomatic recognition, despite the understandings which had been formalised in 1973 and it looked for a while as though relations between the two Germanies would return to the state of the early 1960s. While this did not prove to be the case, the GDR was especially concerned at this time that events in Poland did not spill over into Germany and undermine the stability of the SED. The division in the communist world surfaced also at the 10th Party Congress of April 1981, when clear disapproval of the Soviet presence in Afghanistan and interventionist policies was voiced - especially by Western communist parties and to a lesser extent by other East Europeans - although the SED expressed its customary loyalty towards the Kremlin.

The GDR officially pursues a policy of "demarcation" (Abgrenzung) vis-a-vis West Germany in an effort to emphasise its distinctiveness as a legitimate sovereign nation and to counteract a residual feeling in West Germany that re-unification under the aegis of the Federal Republic remains an appropriate goal. In 1981 the then Federal Chancellor Helmut Schmidt met the East German leader for a summit conference, although the proclamation of martial law in Poland at the same time produced a standstill in inter-German relations which lasted until the accession in March 1983 of a new West German administration under Helmut Kohl.

A strong and increasing link between the two Germanies is the trade between the two countries. Indeed Honecker, in a speech opening the SED Party training school in Dresden in 1977, came close to an apology for this link when he talked of "changes in the international situation", of the "broadening of trade with the West", which was necessary to help the GDR in its programme of socialist construction[6] After the Soviet Union, West Germany is the GDR's largest trading partner and commerce is conducted free of duties, taxes and other restrictions. This, in effect, makes the GDR an unofficial member of the European Community. The GDR derives financial assistance from West Germany in a number of other ways, from direct funding for maintaining and improving the transit routes between West Berlin and the West German border, to support for the inter-German telephone and postal services, and even waste and sewage disposal for West Berlin. Moreover, East Germany enjoys interest-free credit of several million West German Marks per year from the Federal Bank of the FRG which enables the GDR to maintain a virtual permanent overdraft on import-export trade (thus it can import goods from West Germany without having to pay for them immediately). West Germany imports agricultural produce and household appliances from the GDR and uses the arrangement (called the "swing overdraft") to extract political concessions from East Germany. An example of this occurred when Federal Chancellor Kohl approved large loans to the GDR in return for adjustments to the death traps at the border. It is also estimated that the West German government has paid over 3 billion marks since 1971 for the release of prisoners on humanitarian grounds (2676 political prisoners were freed in this way in 1986). Links of this nature have tempted some observers to speak of a "de facto unity" between East and West Germany, although such claims look exaggerated in the light of the two fundamentally different social and political systems and in view of the differing interests which continue to underlie each country's willingness to entertain such links. Predictably, perhaps, West Germans bewail what they see as a one-way financial traffic to the benefit of the East Germans (and, occasionally, to the positive detriment of some West German manufacturers who are being undercut by artificially cheap imports from the GDR), while the East Germans are above all keen to gain access to hard currency and lucrative western markets. For the time being, however, the Federal German government is willing to pay a high financial price for stability in West Berlin and for a degree of influence on humanitarian political issues. It looks, then, as though relations between East and West Germany have settled into a fairly stable mould, occasionally interrupted by relatively minor diplomatic differences or, more seriously, by relations between the major power blocs (e.g. as in 1987 over the question as to what co-operation should take place between East and West Berlin in the celebrations of the city's 750th birthday celebrations). A planned visit to West Germany was repeatedly postponed from 1981 for one reason or another (e.g. because of the deaths of two West German travellers being questioned in the GDR about alleged misconduct, or from 1984 under Soviet pressure arising from the stationing of new nuclear missiles in the West and because of Bonn's support for the US President Reagan's Strategic Defence Initiative which involved the development of new weapons in space). In 1987, however, Honecker stated publicly that it was still "very likely" that he would visit the West eventually. Whether or not the policy of "openness" instigated within the Soviet Union by its new leader, Mikhail Gorbachev, will affect inter-German relations in the longer term is not known yet. Up to the present moment, however, the new Soviet direction has been studiously ignored by the East German leadership which appears to view greater democratisation and openness to the media as unleashing potentially dangerous challenges to its own legitimacy. Once again, as in the last years of the Ulbricht era, it is the presence of the Federal Republic which in part inspires these fears and ironically prompts the very intransigeance which the East German leaders are afraid to renounce.

CHAPTER 5
THE APPARATUS

Western-type democracies are invariably governed by a parliament in which a number of political parties are represented. A typical pattern is for a single party - or perhaps a coalition of parties - to dominate for a period of legislature by virtue of a majority of seats gained in a general election. The parliament is the law-making body (legislature) and is generally independant of the civil service and judiciary which enforce these laws (the impartial executive). The principles of this system have evolved over at least two centuries and embody the key features of the separation of power (legislature v. executive) and political pluralism (different parties representing competing interests). Further essential principles include universal franchise (everyone may vote) and the secret ballot (which ensures that the vote is a free one). Although parliament is the supreme body, control effectively passes to the majority party for its period of power.

This parliamentary system is rejected in Soviet communism as only apparently democratic because it conceals the true domination of capitalistic interests: those who own and control a nation's economic resources and the means of production in reality control its destiny and the superficial choice among parties is held to offer no genuine alternative to this monopoly of power. This belief is used to justify the total control of the country by a single party representing the working population - the so-called "dictatorship of the proletariat". East Germany has more than one political party and in that respect it differs from the Soviet Union where the Communist Party is the sole permitted one. The chapter on the historical development of the GDR, however, explains how these other parties, far from being independant, are allowed alongside the mass organisations purely as "vehicles of transmission" of the SED's policies to sections of the populace to which the traditional German Communist

Party have not historically appealed.

The following section describes briefly how the formal apparatus of government in the GDR operates.

5.1 The People's Chamber (<u>Volkskammer</u>)

The Peoples' Chamber (<u>Volkskammer</u>) is the East German equivalent of parliament and is designated in the constitution as the supreme organ of power in the land. Its current membership is 500 and is re-elected every five years. Apart from the SED, the following parties and mass organisations are represented and comprise the so-called "Democratic Block: the Christian Democratic Union (CDU), the Liberal Democratic Party of Germany (LDPD), the National Democratic Party of Germany (NDPD), the Democratic Peasants' Party of Germany (DBD), the Free German Trade Union Federation (FDGB), the Free German Youth (FDJ), the Cultural Federation of the GDR (KB) and the Democratic Women's Federation of Germany (DFD). The GDR prides itself on having no "full-time professional parliamentarians" as such, for members of parliament remain at their place of work or organisation and can, in theory, be de-elected for gross dereliction of duty. At the election of 1981 the SED received 127 seats, the other parties 52 each, the FDGB 68, the FDJ 40, the DFD 35 and the KB 22. The People's Chamber does not sit very often (18 times between 1971 and 1976, 13 times between 1976 and 1981) and rarely functions as a forum of debate: its role is to approve decisions made elsewhere - usually unanimously - and is largely acclamatory.

The Chamber elects the chairmen and members of two major bodies or councils: the Council of Ministers (<u>Ministerrat</u>) and the Council of State: it also elects the chairman of the National Defence Council, the President, the Judges of the Supreme Court and the Attorney General (<u>Generalstaatsanwalt</u>).The Chamber constitutes numerous committees (14 standing) responsible for various aspects of life and work, onto which not merely members of parliament, but also lay experts can be co-opted.

5.2 The Council of State

The Council of State (Staatsrat) was used by Ulbricht as the main vehicle of legislation and control, although it immediately lost this role on the accession of Honecker. It is no longer the standing representative body of the Volkskammer and does not implement or interpret the constitution. Since 1976, however, when Honecker took over the chairmanship, it was felt that a certain upgrading would occur, although the Council now seems primarily to function as a means of consultation with the mass organisations and parties. Its membership is about 25.

5.3 The Council of Ministers

The powerful Council of Ministers (Ministerrat), whose influence under Ulbricht was restricted mainly to economic affairs, now functions, according to the constitution, as the "government" (Regierung) of the GDR and implements national policy. It has over 40 members from whom are drawn the chairman of the 11 ministries concerned with justice, education, trade, industry, etc. Within the Council exists a 16-strong Presidium of senior members which conducts the day-to-day business.

Important bodies directly responsible to the Council include the State Plan Commission responsible for implementing and overseeing the Five Year Economic Plans, the Council for Agriculture and Food, and the Committee of Worker and Peasant Inspection (Arbeiter- und Bauerninspektion or ABI). The ABI was formed in 1963 as part of the New Economic System: it is also responsible to the Central Committee of the SED and oversees the areas of industry and transport to ensure that they meet productivity targets. It has about 200,000 honorary members throughout the GDR.

5.4 "Bezirke" and "Kreise"

The above constitutes the highest and most central level of administration in the GDR. The 11 ministries represented in the Council of Ministers control the various collective organisations at the middle level, including those for production and industry such as the VVBs, the VEBs, and the "Kombinate". The middle geographical level of admininstration is the Bezirk, or region, of which there are 15 throughout the country, including Berlin: these were created as economic units during the great administrative reform of 1952. The State Plan Commission thus controls the Bezirk Plan Commission and the the Council of Ministers itself oversees the Bezirk Councils which comprise 160 to 200 members each and are responsible for fulfilling national directives and objectives at this level (for example, they translate the national Five Year Plans into regionally implemented yearly plans).

Below the middle level lies the Kreis or Gemeinde (district): the small Bezirk of Suhl, for instance, in the far south western corner of the country, consists of eight constituent "Kreise" plus the city of Suhl itself. Both the Bezirke and "Kreise" are termed "local representative bodies" (örtliche Vertretungen) and operate according to a constitution of local government which was most recently revised in 1985 (previously in 1973). An important function of the local representative bodies is to avoid the inherently negative effect of planning decisions reached far way in a highly centralist state by ensuring that they are implemented and adapted according to local needs and conditions.

The role of the local representative bodies demonstrates crucial aspects of the way in which central plans are enacted in the GDR according to the principle of "democratic centralism" (which is embodied in the SED party statute). First of all, decisions (Beschlüsse) reached at central level tend to take a general form ("what is to be done"), while the practical details ("how to do it") are delegated to local officials and organisations: among other things this can leave considerable freedom for either over-

The Regions (<u>Bezirke</u>) of the GDR

or under-zealous functionaries, but it does avoid total bureacratic constipation. Secondly it reveals how the GDR sees the process as democratic, enabling it to speak of the unity of central state planning and the individual initiative of the citizen' . The point is that what may be the subject of local question or initiative is never the "what" or "why" of the broad decision, but only the "how" of its implementation.

5.5 The SED Party Organisation

The SED exercises a complete and permanent control over the People's Chamber. This control is embodied in the constitution which declares that the GDR is a socialist state and political organisation of workers and peasants under the leadership of "its Marxist-Leninist Party" (Article 1). Although the SED does not have a theoretical overall majority of seats in parliament (in 1981: 127 out of 500), all other parties and organisations in practice acknowledge its leadership and are allied to the SED through "personal union" (i.e. the SED selects and approves their leaders). The system is now so well established that the vestiges of opposition exerted by the historical non-communist parties during the early years of the republic have totally disappeared.

The party is organised according to principles of "territory and production", i.e. has party groups and units in all residential areas/communities and places of work. These number over 80,000 and the total party membership in 1986 consisted of over 2,300,000 million.

5.6 Congress

According to statute the supreme organ of the party is the Party Congress, which meets every five years (the 11th Congress gathered in April 1986). The Congress is a well-rehearsed festival - often attended by foreign communist parties and even the Soviet leadership - at which formal expressions of unity and socialist brotherliness are expressed at great length by (in 1986) over 2500 delegates and representatives. The political direction for the future is announced, alongside the next Five Year Plan.

5.7 The Central Committee

The Congress also chooses the Central Committee (Zentralkomite or ZK) which comprises over 150 members and functions as a kind of executive committee for the Congress, determining the general political direction and sending party representatives to all areas of the state apparatus as well as selecting candidates for the People's Chamber. The Central Committee is bound to meet half-yearly but in practice does so about four times a year. Even so, the relative infrequency of its meetings suggests that its prime function is to implement decisions reached in the inner recesses of the party. The access of its members to both the party leaders and the state apparatus, however, along with the fact that in past crises it has swiftly become a forum of discussion would also indicate that it has considerable influence and is privy to critical information. Various specialist commissions, for example, on national security and agitation, as well as central research and educational institutions, are responsible to the Central Committee.

5.8 The Politbureau

From the Central Committee's ranks is selected the Politbureau, which meets weekly under the chairmanship of the Party Leader and undertakes the day-to-day political leadership at the very highest and most secret level. Although in recent times the membership of the Politbureau has fallen slightly, it comprised between 1981 and 1986 17 full members and 8 candidates (these are usually approved as full members in the course of time). The Politbureau has it own Bureau or Office which attends to the technical servicing of the main organisation and performs the preparatory work for meetings, and each member of the Politbureau has his own personal secretary. Very little is known of how the Politbureau functions in detail except that much personal consultation among members probably takes place outside actual meetings, at which the decisions are reached, usually by concensus and not through votes. Information for meetings can be prepared by members themselves, by "Specialist Commissions" or more usually by the Secretariat of the Central Committee (see below), although each member represents an area of expertise in which only the General Secretary himself would normally feel competent to intervene. There is no area, either personal or political, trivial or important, that the Politbureau would consider outside its sphere of deliberation.

5.9 The Secretariat of the Central Committee

The Secretariat of the Central Committee consists of approximately 11 Central Committee members who are also in the Politbureau. They stand at the head of a large "apparatus" (about 2000 staff) which oversees the implementation of the party's directives in the various organs of state and in the country as a whole. The apparatus comprises over 40 departments whose influence extends down to the local party organisation. Alongside the Politbureau the Secretariat is the most powerful committee of the SED determining the daily running of the party at the most senior level and preparing material and reports for the Politbureau. It draws up the Five Year Plans for consideration by the Bureau and serves as the main channel for their implementation lower down the ladder.

In addition the Central Secretariat is responsible for the selection and progress of the party "cadres" - the local party units present in all factories, schools, universities, etc - and determines staffing at the higher levels of the party apparatus itself (down to Kreis-leaders), including posts in ministries, the economy, industry, diplomatic service, and the sciences - the so-called "nomenclature". It is estimated that about half a million SED members belong to the nomenclature and occupy senior posts throughout the land.

Despite purges and personnel changes (mostly before 1958) only 69 persons were Politbureau members between 1946 and 1984 and hence masters of the destiny of the GDR. In the early days, up till about the 1960s, most were long standing communists with bitter experiences of the Hitler period, but younger party leaders now predominate.

5.10 The Control Commission

A further central party institution is the Central Party Control Commission which is a kind of internal party police. The Commission is responsible for discipline and may even expel miscreants. Set up in 1948 as part of the re-organisation of the SED into a tightly disciplined "New Type Party", its functions were to combat "enemies" of the party, corruption, abuse of official position, and "slander of leading party members", etc. Its decisions must be ratified by the Central Committee and are binding on the rank-and-file membership.

The Control Commission consisted in 1984 of one chairman, his representative, seven members and six candidate members, although parallel sub-control commissions exist at each administrative level of the party organisation, from Bezirk to Kreis.

5.11 Membership

Since its formation in 1946 the SED has changed both in numbers of members and the structure of its membership. At the very first, a concerted recruitment campaign pushed membership up from about 1.3 million in 1948 to 2 million in an effort to swamp the influence of the residual Social Democratic element left over from the merger with the more moderate party. From 1948 to 1953, however, members dropped sharply (1.23 million in

1953), especially as entry into the party was restricted to workers and other social groups were excluded. Despite the ongoing policy of promoting working class membership, numbers have steadily climbed to well over 2 million once again (after 1976). According to social origin (as opposed to present occupation) over 72% of all SED members were working class in 1983 - if official statistics are to be believed. In terms of age the SED is quite a youthful party, with about one half of its members under 40, and a significant proportion under 30.

CHAPTER 6
GEOGRAPHY AND NATURAL RESOURCES

6.1 Boundaries

The GDR is entirely a creation of the Second World War. During the course of the war it became clear to the allies (USA, USSR, UK) that the German Reich would have to be occupied for a period - perhaps two years - and that boundaries for zones of occupation for each allied power were required. The present western boundary was drawn up at a conference in Quebec in 1944 - "rather hastily", in the words of Winston Churchill[8] - and the eastern frontier with Poland was decided at the end of the war in 1945 at the conferences of Yalta and Potsdam. At the time, however, these boundaries were never intended to be more than provisional measures for it was assumed that sooner or later the zones would be reconstituted into a future reunited Germany. That the division has become permanent, however, is due to the conflict of interests between the Western allies (Britain and America) and the Soviet Union, with each incorporating its respective half of Germany into its own ideological system and power bloc.

The eastern boundary of the GDR follows the Rivers Oder and Neiße, which form a line running from the Baltic Sea in the north, southwards to the border with Czechoslovakia. Comparison with the historical German frontiers reveals that this represents a considerable loss of territory to Poland which had existed eastwards of this line. The reason for this is political. Since the Soviet Union had agreed with Hitler before the war that an area of eastern Poland should go to Russia (the Poles did not have much say in the deal) it was now agreed that Poland should be recompensed, not with the original territory, but with land from conquered Germany. The Oder-Neiße is at least a natural geographical boundary, however, except for a small area near the Baltic coast where the frontier moves westwards to carefully exclude

The Major Physical Features of the GDR

Major Rivers and Towns of the GDR

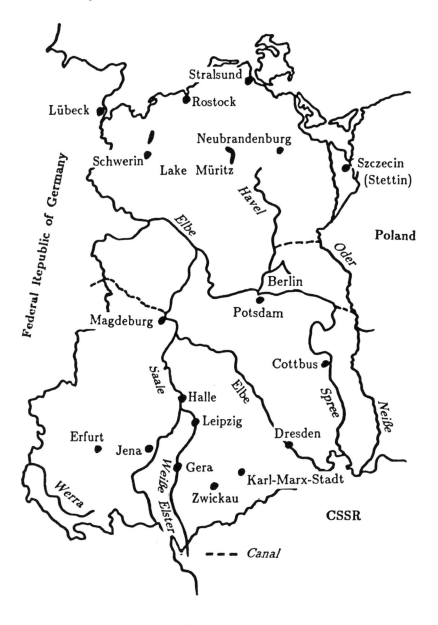

the former major German port of Stettin from German control.

If the Oder-Neiße line is at least a natural geographical demarcation, then the opposite is true for the western boundary. This was actually drawn in line with traditional German administrative areas, but rarely follows any natural geographical or historical features. It begins in the Bay of Lübeck, just east of the port of Lübeck itself, runs down to the River Elbe, which it follows upstream for about 60 miles before taking a winding and tortuous route southwards to the north-western tip of Czechoslovakia.

On its southern side, the GDR faces Czechoslovakia. This frontier has existed since the Middle Ages and follows the summit of the Erzgebirge mountain range.

The total area of the GDR thus encompassed comprises 42000 square miles (108,780 square km).

6.2 Landforms

Most of the country lies within the great North European Plain, which stretches from the Netherlands across North Germany into the Soviet Union. This plain was subject to glaciation, especially in the more northerly parts which are characterised in East Germany by the presence of moraines (debris deposited by the moving ice sheets), large aprons of outwash sands (formed while the glaciers were at a temporary standstill), and the primeval valleys of the Rivers Elbe, Havel and Spree, which were originally cut out by water from the melting ice.

In more detail, the Baltic Coast, from the Bay of Lübeck to the Stettin Bay, is low and flat with some shallow cliffs in places. There is also an area of narrow, complex channels and offshore islands, especially around Rügen. The coast is very sandy with numerous sandbars and dunes.

Just south of the Baltic coastal region the land is low and rolling with some lakes and small marshes. It gently rises to the south towards the Mecklenburg Lake Plateau, which stretches virtually right across the country from east to west and is from 10 to 25 miles wide. Here, hills are low but steep, with numerous marshes and lakes in between. The largest of the lakes are those of Schwerin and Müritz. It is a distinctive region, famous as the German "lakeland" and covered with more water than any other part of the country.

The outwash area to the south of the Mecklenburg plateau slopes down to the river valleys and consists largely of sandy soil now covered with forests.

The river valleys themselves form a broad belt which cuts from west to east right across the country. The principal rivers of this belt are the Elbe, Havel and Spree, of which the largest is the Elbe, rising beyond the south eastern corner of the GDR and flowing right across to end in the North Sea, just beyond Hamburg in West Germany. The river belt consists of several marshy valleys, broken by the central heathland of the Fläming. In the north eastern part of the area, north of the Fläming, lies Berlin and the historical region of Brandenburg, which represented march territory confronting the Slavs to the east during the Middle Ages and became the centre of Prussian and pan-German power in the nineteenth century. As for the soil, the heathland is covered mostly with a sandy loam and the area around Berlin is, likewise, sandy, with pine plantations.

Immediately to the south of the primeval river valleys - which represent the limit of the residual effects of glaciation - lie, in the west, the Harz mountains and, to the south, the mountain range called the Erzgebirge, through which runs the border with Czechoslovakia. Between the valley of the Elbe and the Harz mountains is a low, undulating plateau most of which is covered with loess (a mixture of fine sand and clay). The region is fertile, treeless, easily traversed and has given rise to the historically important and prosperous nearby cities of

Madgeburg, Halle and Leipzig. Included in this area, just west and south of Magdeburg, which is situated on the Elbe, just before it turns sharply northwards between the Fläming and the extension of the Lüneburger Heide, is the so-called Magdeburger Börde, where the loess is especially deep and extensive.

As the Harz itself is approached, the soil becomes lighter and less fertile. The mountain range is about 784 square miles (of which two thirds lie inside West Germany), extending for about 50 miles with a width of 15 to 20 miles and with altitudes of over 3000 ft (highest mountain is the Brocken of 3747 ft). It is an imposing range, very different from the surrounding landscape and rising steeply from the lowlands on most sides except the south east: for this reason it has played an important role in German folklore with strong associations of the supernatural. More prosaically, however, it was historically a source of minerals and iron-ore, although now only copper-mining is significant.

To the south of the Harz lies the Thuringian Basin, an area of hilly lowland bounded further to the south by the mountainous Thuringian Forest. The Basin, through which flows the River Unstrut, is mainly limestone with loess. The soil can be extremely rich here and the basin has given rise to some of the earliest signs of urban development in Germany (Gotha, Erfurt, Weimar, Jena).

South of the Thuringian Basin lies the Forest of Thuringia, which is a long and narrow ridge extending about 50 miles and attaining heights of 3000 ft, where summer grazing takes place on open grassy levels. Most of the area, however, is forested with conifers. The ridge of the Thuringian Forest continues in a south easterly direction into the great forests of Franconia (in Bavaria) and Bohemia (CSSR), but directly adjacent to the eastern section of Thuringian Forest itself the land widens out into a broad slate plateau, cut through in places by river valleys (the Saale and the Weisse Elster) which are deep, narrow and carry railway lines. On the plateau there is little agriculture, some hydro-electric power and quarrying, while forests of birch and spruce predominate. The northern side of the plateau drops down to below 1600 ft, while, towards the south, it rises to over 2000 ft before plunging steeply into the valley of the River Eger which lies beyond the GDR frontier inside Czech territory. The plateau region has historically been known as the Vogtland in German.

The highest southern portion of the plateau constitutes the Erzgebirge mountain range - the GDR/Czech border follows the ridge line - which extends northwestwards for 140 miles from the Fichtelgebirge mountains in the south west corner of the country. Within the Erzgebirge range and in a line due south of Karl-Marx Stadt lies East Germany's highest mountain peak, the Fichtelberg (over 4000 ft). The Erzgebirge supports little or no agriculture, being forested and maintaining near arctic conditions at the summits. The name itself, however, means "ore mountains" and they are or have been rich in lead, zinc, silver, tin and other minerals. From the Middle Ages until the discovery of the New World silver was extensively mined by the famous Függer family until cheaper sources were discovered across the Atlantic.

The Erzgebirge continues at its northerly end into the mountains of the Lausitz, but not before being cut through deeply by the valley of the River Elbe. This narrow valley is famous as an area of such outstanding natural beauty that it has acquired the title of the Saxon Switzerland. To the north west the valley opens out into the basin of Saxony and to the south east the great basin of Bohemia: the valley thus represents the pass from one basin into the other through the Erzgebirge-Lausitz mountain chain. Short tributaries of the Elbe have cut back into the valley sides to form isolated or grouped flat topped mountains with steep and forested sides. The valley floor itself undulates and is well cultivated. Slightly to the north and east of the Lausitz we pick up the River Neiße which runs north for approximately 80 miles before flowing into the Oder which continues for another 100 miles to reach the Baltic at the Polish port of Szczecin (formerly German Stettin).

About 50 miles north of the Fichtelberg in the Erzgebirge lies an elongated basin which contains East Germany's only real sources of bituminous coal. The output is small but was enough to lead the establishment of the industrial cities of Karl-Marx-Stadt (formerly Chemnitz) and Zwickau in the nineteenth century.

6.3 Climate

Stretching from the Baltic Sea in the north for almost 300 miles southward into the central European continent, East Germany experiences a range of climatic conditions extending from British-type mild, wet winters and cool summers in the north, to the cold, frosty winters and hot dry summers characterstic of continental climates in the south. Over and above this general picture, individual geographical features mould the climate locally, so that, for example, the Harz mountains have a greater rainfall throughout the year, while the Thuringian Basin is one of the driest areas in Germany, followed by eastern Mecklenburg and the valley of the Oder. Snow lies for the longest periods in the east and south and on the mountains while ice forms on the Elbe for about 3 weeks in the year: the Baltic is usually ice-free except for extremely severe winters, when pack ice can render the coast land-locked (e.g as in the exceptionally severe winter of 1946/47). The average January temperature for Leipzig, in the south, is -8'C, while, on the northern coast, it hovers just below freezing point.

6.4 Vegetation

If most of present-day East Germany was covered with forests at the time of the Roman Empire, the introduction of superior wheeled ploughs and, with this, a rapid growth in the settled population during the Middle Ages up until the fourteenth century, radically altered the character of the landscape. Forests and woodland were cleared, the fertile areas of loess were cultivated and even the inferior good soils of Saxony and Mecklenburg were exploited. In the eighteenth century, the wet marshland of Brandenburg was drained and the rivers and channels brought under control for land utilisation. The forests of the mountain areas remained, especially those of Thuringia and the Erzgebirge, although much of the original hardwoods have been depleted through human exploitation over hundreds of years and replaced by softwood conifers. Further extensive forests are to be found on the light soils of the regions just north of the primeval valleys of the Elbe, Havel and Spree rivers and in Brandenburg: these are man-made and entirely coniferous.

6.5 Agriculture

Although eastern Germany, especially after the war, was regarded by many as a primarily agriculural region, it cannot be said to be rich in farmland. One third of the soil is sandy, much of the north is either heavy clay or sandy heathland, while the primeval river valleys yield ground which is often too wet to support good crops. And, of course, over a quarter of the land area is given over to woodland and forest. High quality and fertile soil accounts for only about 7% of the total area of the GDR and the common pattern of agriculture has been to farm large areas in order to generate relatively small yields. Nevertheless 58% of the total land area is given over to farming of one kind or another, although, in common with other industrialised nations, there is a steady annual decrease in the amount of land available for farming as it is given over for manufacturing or industrial purposes. Compared to the Federal Republic, the GDR has twice as much land per inhabitant available for agriculture, although this is small compared with other socialist countries. The best cropland lies towards the south, on the light loess soils around Magdeburg, Halle, Leipzig and Erfurt but the sandy regions elsewhere are often capable of supporting crops. Rye is the most important single crop and is grown nearly everywhere, especially, however, in the sandy areas around Potsdam and Frankfurt in the east and on the clay of Neubrandenburg and Schwerin. Wheat thrives on the best soils, the so-called "black earth", of Halle, Magdeburg and the Thuringian Basin. Potatoes are a staple diet in East Germany and have the advantage of being able to grow on soils of varying quality. Sugar beet production has increased since the 1960s and serves the export market.

Animal stock has been greatly developed since before the Second World War, especially cattle, pigs and poultry (sheep less so, despite attempts to foster them for the textile industry).

The programme of collectivisation of farming resources has, of course, had a dramatic effect on the agricultural economy. The speed at which the programme was pushed through in the later 1950s considerably reduced the nation's farming efficiency, while the deliberate stress on industrialisation exacerbated the deficit: thus, for example, the so-called "industrial crops", oilseed rape and sugar beet, have been promoted at the expense of foodstuffs for direct human consumption. Overall East Germany remains a net food importer, especially in the areas of vegetables and fruit.

Settlement patterns were also markedly altered by the collectivisation programme. At the end of the war eastern Germany inherited the historical pattern of a predominance of very large rural estates in the hands of a small number of rich landowners (remnants of the old Prussian aristocracy), especially in the north: smaller holdings prevailed in the south. With the disinheritance of the big landowners, which took place in September 1945 and amidst popular approval - the pattern of ownership abruptly changed, although it was not until the early 1960s that this extended to most areas of agricultural life: if one third of the total cropland was collectivised by the 1945 measure, over 90% had been converted to new patterns of ownership by 1961. With the establishment of collectives the traditional village ceased to be a group of individual farms, and the abandoned buildings were either dismantled or re-used for other purposes. Multi-story apartment blocks even appeared to house employees of the collective. A look at a plan of a typical small village

would show that a small number of large fields has
replaced the many long, narrow strips and enclosed
meadows, while a few, often modern buildings serve to
house animals, milk cows, store grain and feed and
maintain machinery for the whole collective.
Collectivisation and mechanisation have furthermore
reduced the need for labour.

6.6 Population and Resources

Since reaching a peak of about 20 million at the end
of the Second World War (pushed up by an influx of
returning prisoners of war and refugees who had fled or
been expelled from former German territories in Eastern
Europe) the GDR has declined in population. The decline
became catastrophic as citizens - especially the young and
well educated - escaped to the more prosperous West
until the exodus was halted by the Berlin Wall in 1961.
Thereafter from 1962 until 1968 the population became
much less mobile and even increased very slightly but has
been slowly dropping since the 1970s. This is a
phenomenon common to north European industrial
countries and is assisted in the GDR by the strong
pressures and incentives for women to work. At present
around seventeen million are permanently resident in the
GDR.

The population is concentrated in those regions which
have the most intensive agriculture and industry. Thus
nearly 2 million people live in the highly industrialised
Karl-Marx-Stadt area, followed by Halle-Saale, Dresden,
Leipzig, Erfurt, Magdeburg and Berlin (in 1982 almost 1.2
million inhabitants were registered in East Berlin). Urban
density is greatest in Berlin, which, along with Cottbus,
Frankfurt an der Oder and Rostock are experiencing
population increases. The rural population is sparsest in
the agriculturally poor areas directly north and south of
Berlin and the Elbe-Havel-Spree river valley belt. It is
densest in the Magdeburger Börde, the central Thuringian
Basin and on the fertile forelands of the Erzgebirge and
the Lausitz. Overall the GDR is a predominantly urban

and industrial nation with over three quarters of its citizens living in communities of 2000 or more members and one third distributed among the 15 large cities (defined as communities of over 100,000).

After the Second World War the GDR suffered from a chronic maldistribution of its human resources from an economic point of view, with an especially acute shortage of young men of working age: the manpower shortage left over from the carnage of the war itself was exacerbated, of course, by the spontaneous outflow of citizens to the West. Thus, as late as 1970, only 58% of the population was of working age, 23% were under the age of fifteen, and 20% were pensioners. Since then, however, the trend has begun to improve, with the figures for 1982 comprising 64% of working age, 19% children and 17% pensioners. What is characteristic of the GDR is that a very high proportion of the potential workforce is actually engaged in work and that 50% of this proportion is female. Thus, for the end of 1982, of 10.7 million people of working age, 8.8 million have jobs, of whom 4.5 are men and 4.3 are women. The number of births in the GDR sank dramatically from the early 1960s by nearly 50% towards the mid-1970s (1961: 300,818, 1973: 180,336), but recovered somewhat by the beginning of the 1980s (1980: 245,132), probably as a result of superior social provisions for families and working mothers and success in reducing the infant mortality rate. The official policy is to increase the productive population through encouraging larger families (from the present one or two children to three or four as a rule), although to achieve this various long-term social policies and changes in human attitudes may be necessary for which the data and methods do not yet exist. The GDR government, however, is conscious of the problem and fully intends to tackle it within the context of further development of the socialist way of life.

6.7 Industry

The industrial problems confronting post-war East Germany were considerable. Apart from the war-damage itself and the Soviet policy of extracting reparations in the form of raw materials and current production, it had little high quality fuel and lacked a modern iron and steel industry. Furthermore it had no developed sea ports and possessed the remains of an east-west orientated transport system instead of the north-south network now required. On the balance side it retained considerable resources of low-grade fuel and mineral salts and not least a highly-trained, well disciplined and experienced workforce.

Bituminous coal (Steinkohle) as found in the West German Ruhr and near Hannover is required for iron and steel production and for the building and chemical industries. Although it may occur geologically in the GDR it is too inaccessible to mine, so that production, which in 1958 was nearly 3 million tons, had virtually ceased by 1977. In 1982 the requirement of about 8 million tons was met by imports from the USSR, Poland and Czechoslovakia. The lack of quality bituminous coal has been a great burden to industrial development in the GDR.

The geologically younger and less efficient brown coal or lignite (Braunkohle), however, occurs in adundance in the GDR, which has the world's largest reserves of this commodity (about one third). It is easy to extract, being both accessible from the surface and present in very thick seams, although it contains too much moisture (as much as 62%) when mined and needs "briquetting" - i.e. to be dried and compressed - at the pit-head in order to be useful as a burning agent. The most significant reserves are around Leipzig and in Lausitz and the Cottbus district. The huge opencast mining operations, while economically advantageous, have resulted in much damage to the environment and to agricultural land, although the GDR is attempting to reverse the detrimental effects of this type of mineral exploitation. The high water content of the coal and the opencast environment mean that frost readily disrupts production, while its low calorific value renders transportion over long distances unprofitable. Brown coal is nevertheless the largest single energy source within the GDR and is likely to remain so for the foreseeable future. Production has been steadily increased, from 137 million tons in 1950 to 226 million in 1960 and 276 million in 1982. Over 60% of the raw brown coal thus produced is used in nearby power stations and 37% converted to briquettes at special pit-head processing plants. Extracting and converting brown coal is a fairly new industry and techniques are still under development. The famous "Gas Combine Black Pump" (Gaskombinat Schwarze Pumpe) near Hoyerswerda in the south east is the largest brown coal refining complex in the GDR. Begun in 1956 and using about 70 million tons of coal annually from the nearby Lausitz fields it produces briquettes for industrial and domestic consumption, special high temperature coking coal for use in the chemical and metallurgical industries, and, finally, fully two thirds of city gas for the entire GDR.

Although the GDR possesses and has developed reserves of natural gas at Salzwedel in the west near its border with the Federal Republic, the gas itself is not of high quality and its exploitation stagnated between 1974 and the early 1980s. From 1973, however, the GDR has been supplied with high quality gas from the Soviet Union by means of a pipeline across the border with the CSSR. A similar pipeline, called "Friendship", which enters the GDR near Schwedt at the border with Poland in the north east, also provides most of the oil imported: this, too, comes from the Soviet Union. These pipelines demonstrate the GDR's economic integration into the Eastern Bloc.

Since the Five Year Plan for 1981-85 the GDR has pursued a rigorous policy of energy conservation and rationalisation in order to reduce its import requirements. In practice this policy takes the form of price sanctions against concerns and plants which exceed stated consumption norms (they may pay up to ten times as much for the excess energy), strict controls and inspections of energy use, price increases for industry, reductions in permitted room temperatures, a programme of railway electrification and the transfer of freight from road to rail and waterways.

Further mining industries include potash, uranium, lead, zinc and copper. The iron and steel smelting industry (for which almost 2 million tons of iron ore was imported in 1982) was rapidly built up as a national priority directly after the war and is now situated primarily at Eisenhüttenstadt in the east, Brandenburg and Henningsdorf (both near Berlin), and various other centres in the south. At present the metal industry is in the process of modernisation and is switching from its earlier energy-intensive emphasis on bulk iron and steel production to higher quality steels.

The GDR's main industrial activities encompass engineering, chemicals, car manufacturing and shipbuilding, textiles and clothing, and glass and ceramics. It also has an extensive electro-technical base and manufactures high precision optical instruments. With the exception of shipbuilding and some light engineering, most of the industry is concentrated in the southern half of the country.

6.8 Private Enterprise

Although almost all manufacturing and industrial activity in the GDR is state-owned and conforms to the socialist principle of common ownership, some sections of the economy remain in private hands and co-exist with the centralised system. This is actually true of the economies of all socialist countries, with differences, however, in the degree to which private enterprise is tolerated: the general principle is that private activities exist and can even be encouraged in order to bridge gaps and deficiencies which the state-owned enterprises either cannot or at present do not choose to meet. Of course, the scale of activity is controlled and subject to official licencing.

Thus, in 1977 in the GDR, there existed almost 94,000 small private concerns employing over a quarter of a million people and accounting for over 63% of technical repair and service work, especially for domestic needs, which has always been well below western standards. Another important area is the catering and restaurant industry, of which 43% was in private control in 1977. Furthermore, the state acknowledged in 1976 the importance of private suppliers in distributing food and essential day-to-day goods, especially in residential and rural areas, by granting more licences in this area. Material support, incentives and even provision for apprentice training was also extended to private concerns engaged in small trades. The encouragement and co-existence of private business was incorporated into the national economic plan for 1976-1980 and was granted considerable financial resources.

6.9 Communications

War and occupation inflicted severe damage upon the entire communications network of the GDR. The sudden re-orientation from east-west to north-south produced a host of new requirements needing resources for investment and re-development which the nation did not possess. Not until the end of the 1960s and early 1970s did the state embark on a serious programme of modernisation and extension of the road and rail network, which had been grossly neglected, partly through the decision to concentrate on new heavy industrial centres. Lack of adequate transport facilities produced frequent supply and bottleneck problems for the entire economy. Still scarce investment resources are now concentrated on the two major means of communication, the railways and the road network (the ratio of funding is 50% to 20-25%, reflecting the order of priority).

War-related damage to the railway network of eastern Germany meant that, when lines were restored in 1946, only 60% of stock which had existed in 1936 remained, with locomotives and goods waggons being in particularly short supply. Apart from the line connecting Berlin with the east, all twin tracks were reduced to single lines as part of Soviet reparations (not restored until 1952 onwards). The most far-reaching consequence, however, was undoubtedly the severance of all but a few lines with the west for military, goods and passenger use - especially to preserve the links between West Berlin and the Federal Republic, the so-called "transit traffic" (Transitverkehr).

With the division of Germany, a certain re-distribution of population took place, with people moving away from the formerly important border areas with the west and the population of the northern coastal towns increasing. As a result passenger and freight requirements moved abruptly to the north-south axis. The GDR's rail network is the densest in Eastern Europe with most lines concentrated in the populous and industrial south (Karl-Marx-Stadt, Dresden and Leipzig), although Berlin remains the radial focal point for the country as a whole. Recent years have seen a drive towards containerisation, electrification and the establishment of inter-city express services linking the ten district capitals with East Berlin. The expansion of main freight and passenger services goes hand in hand with an overall policy of rationalisation of the network, entailing closures of uneconomic stretches. Every large industrial concern in the GDR, however, is intended to have its own railway link.

6.10 Roads

Road building has never enjoyed a high priority for the transport planners of the GDR and the national network has suffered as a consequence. Inadequate links and poor road surfaces remain a common picture, which is unlikely to improve as efforts are concentrated on saving energy costs by improving the rail and water transport network. Significant new highways have been constructed since the war, however, in particular Dresden-Leipzig (1971), Berlin-Rostock (1978), and the Berlin Ringway (1979). Upgrading of the Berlin-Hamburg and Berlin-Helmstedt transit routes (completed in the early 1980s) has been made possible through the financial assistance of the West German government.

6.11 Waterways

The waterway system of the GDR is more useful for east-west transit traffic than internal tansport and cannot take the largest barges of the West German rivers and canals. Nonetheless it makes a significant contribution to the internal movement of freight and is earmarked for development. The system is about 900 miles long and consists principally of the River Elbe running south east to north west and a canal linking the western and eastern borders. Although all the major navigable rivers, including the Elbe, Havel, Saar and Oder are linked, East Germany's major port, Rostock, is not yet attached to the existing waterway network, although such a connection has been long planned and would represent an invaluable link with the industrial south. At the moment even the busiest parts of the system are utilised to only 50% of their total potential capacity, with the largest internal harbours at Magdeburg (the crossing point of the east-west canal and the Elbe), Frankfurt (Oder), Dresden, Berlin, Potsdam and Halle.

All aspects of waterway traffic and maintainance of the network is controlled by a single central organisation, the Combine for Internal Waterway Traffic (Kombinat Binnenschiffahrt und Wasserstrassen), formed in 1979 in Berlin. In 1982 this had 1161 vessels/barges, with a total capacity of over 600 000 tons.

6.12 Ports

The GDR possesses three sea ports of economic significance, Rostock, Wismar and Stralsund. The largest and most important is by far Rostock, with good rail and motorway links, which is roughly on a par with West Germany's second largest port of Bremen-Bremerhaven. A general-purpose port, it specialises in oil and chemicals and is linked by pipelines with the chemical industry centres of Schwedt and Leuna. 80% of the GDR's sea-bound foreign trade passes through Rostock. Wismar handles smaller goods, timber, rolled steel and potash, while

Stralsund serves small vessels trading with the Baltic countries. The GDR is rapidly expanding the capacities of its harbours, especially Rostock, in order to lessen its dependance on foreign ports, notably Hamburg. It should not be forgotten that, before the war, Rostock was never a major port after its medievel heyday. It development since 1945/49 has necessitated the construction of a completely new harbour area away from the town. The merchant naval fleet of the GDR stood at 174 ships in 1983, including 6 tankers and 12 container ships and 8 roll-on roll-off vessels. This represents one sixth of the size of the West German fleet.

CHAPTER 7
ECONOMIC PLANNING

The nature of economic planning in the GDR is part and parcel of the historical and political progress of the country since 1949. The reader is therefore advised to refer to the chapter on the general historical development of East Germany. The section on the theory and evolution of communism and on the principles of socialist ownership of the means of economic production is also recommended. This section will concentrate on the mechanisms of the planned socialist economy in the GDR and review the various plans and strategies adopted up to the present day.

A socialist planned economy has two main aims. These are to overcome the social and structural injustices that have occurred historically in a system where private interests predominate and, secondly, to exploit most effectively national resources and technological advances for the material and cultural benefit of humanity. From the first aim ensues the need for an end to private ownership of large-scale capital and the second can only be achieved through long-term planning on a national scale. To what extent these theoretical intentions are realised or are actually incompatible with a free market economy in which the state functions more as a regulator than an all-pervasive planner may be decided by the reader. The principle of planning, however, is anchored in the national constitution and has been so since 1949 ("The people's economy of the German Democratic Republic is a socialist planned economy").

Economic planning in the GDR is a complex process, involving various authorities, time scales, main plans and sub-plans, and occupying both the highest and the lowest levels of administration, not to mention the daily lives and work of the people. Although the plan concept embraces most social activities, it focusses naturally on economic matters. The implementation of the plan is achieved through the classic economic "levers" of price levels, incentive schemes, interest rates and taxation as well as through straightforward directives, although the balance between these two approaches has varied in the history of the GDR. There are, of course, problems in making a fully planned economy work successfully. The main difficulties arise from uncertainty about the future (e.g. international price fluctuations, energy costs, military policies) and from the need for complete and reliable information on which forward planning decisions can be based. The GDR is attempting to improve the quality of its data gathering and hence the value of its long-term policy formation. There are also difficulties of incentive and workforce motivation. Despite the ideological position that the interests of the workforce and the general population are identical with the central planning authority (in effect, the SED), a great deal of propaganda is expended in attempting to convince the individual that he is a creative, active part of the plan instead of its dull instrument. Plans have the status of legal obligations at factory and practical levels and consultation takes place, not on whether the plan is to be fulfilled or not, but solely on how the targets are to be met. Having said that, a plan does not consist of a crude series of production norms, but will include a complex set of directives and recommendations designed to co-ordinate numerous agencies and attain stated benefits.

7.1 Who is involved in the planning process?

Three levels of planning organisation are commonly recognised. At the highest, or central level all the most important organs of authority are involved. In particular these include the Politbureau of the Central Committee of the SED, the Council of Ministers and the Industry Ministries themselves. The activities and representations of these organs are co-ordinated by a single body, the State Planning Commission, which carries the main burden of working out, presenting and implementing agreed plans. The major aspects of an ecomonic plan will cover the production and use of national resources, investment and consumption levels, rate of growth, economic structure and priorities, co-operation and co-ordination of different areas of production, regional policies, promotion of scientific and technological applications as well as foreign trade (especially co-ordination with the economies of other socialist countries).

On the middle level, Regional Planning Commissions (Bezirksplankommissionen) and the industrial combines (Kombinate, representing groupings of individual plants and factories) will concentrate on working out in concrete terms and in the light of their regional or particular resources the requirements of the plan.

Finally, the lowest tier involves individual factories and local communities who are required to fulfil the plan's terms at a personal and group level according to the resources available to them.

7.2 What types of plan exist?

The "longest term" plan is the so-called "Perspective Plan" (Perspektivplan), which aims at levels of co-ordinated production and social development for the entire Eastern Bloc over a period of 15 to 20 years. At the moment the GDR lies within the perspective plan for the period 1976 - 1990, which is divided into 5-year segments. Such an extended perspective is all the more vulnerable to the problems of inadequate information and inability to react to unforeseen factors which shorter term plans experience, and it is not surprising that the status of the perspective plan is disputed at factory and plant level.

The perspective plan comprises shorter medium term 5-year plans, which in turn are realised through one-year plans for individual admininstrative areas, communities, factories, plants, etc. Since 1976 efforts have been made to move away from yearly planning cycles altogether and co-ordinate everything within terms of the five-year periods 1976-1980 and 1981-1985. The main reason for this shift is to enhance the central control mechanisms but it has not been possible to implement the new policy for smaller units at local and regional level. Since even the overall 5-year plans are subject to revision during their course, it is evident that the techniques of total planning are not yet fully evolved.

The 5-Year Plan announces for the coming five year period the national policy which is to be followed on industrial and agricultural production, the direction of scientific research and development, foreign trade (especially with the CMEA), education and training, the promotion of the interests of young people and women, health, welfare and culture. It can be seen how all-embracing the plan is and how it extends beyond purely economic and manufacturing activities.

The single year plans are the legally binding concrete realisations of the more general strategy. They concentrate on the annual production figures, the deployment of capital, investments and rationalisation, export-import arrangements with the CMEA alongside organisation of the workforce and the provision of wages and salaries. In all practical repects the plans for the year are more detailed versions for specific areas and regions of the various aspects of the parent plan.

The plan for a factory or combine is drawn up for a year or quarter-year. It in turn comprises sub-plans determining volume and quality of output, modernisation procedures, use of resources, investment and financing policies, costing, as well as mobility of the workforce and working hours.

Further specific sub-plans of the overall 5-year parent plan include those for science and technology (since 1977 priority has been assigned to promoting microelectronics and robotic automation in industry) and for territorial or area planning (Territorialplanung). The main function of area planning is the proper location and distribution of industries (including the privately owned concerns) and it has the power at local level to support and promote new ventures. Housing policy, facilities, schools and environmental matters also come under the aegis of area planning, which has greatly increased in importance in recent years and is co-ordinated with general plans for traffic, communications and building.

7.3 Plans since 1948

Long-term and large-scale economic planning in eastern Germany began in 1948 with the setting up of the German Economic Commission (Deutsche Wirtschaftskommission) which was responsible for the entire Soviet Zone and was a forerunner of the later GDR government. Within the context of post-war recovery the Commission drew up a half-year plan for July to December 1948 which affected only the basic raw materials industry and set percentage-based increased production targets.

The 2-Year Plan 1949-1950 was the first truly comprehensive plan which envisaged massive investments to either construct or re-build the heavy iron and steel industry. Engineering and tractor-manufacture was also included, with a total planned increase in industrial production of 110% above that of 1936. Such a target was based on an wholly inadequate assessment of the country's actual production capacity.

The first 5-Year Plan 1951-1955 continued the building up of the iron, steel, chemical and brown coal industries at the cost of consumer goods. The aim was a doubling of the 1950 level of industrial production. The collectivisation of agriculture was announced (1952) and many farmers and peasants left the land. The plan was altered four times (partly as a result of integration with the CMEA, founded in 1949) and failed to achieve its targets: in particular insufficient raw materials were produced to service the engineering and processing industries. 1953 saw the national workers' uprising.

The next 5-Year Plan for 1956-1960 required an

increase of 20% in industrial activity. A second currency reform (1957) was supposed to end rationing, although coal and potatoes remained under limited issue. The build-up of heavy industry continued, however, with the further addition of the GDR's first atomic reactor and the development of the Baltic ports. The GDR ditched this plan in 1958 when the crisis-ridden USSR abandoned its own economic plan, and turned immediately to a new, 7-Year Plan.

The 7-Year Plan for 1959-1965 was one of the most grandiose ever, designed to realise Ulbricht's famous claim of catching up with West Germany by 1961 and demonstrating once and for all the superiority of the socialist system. Production of raw materials would increase by 90%, engineering by 110%, and consumer goods by 84%. Farmland would also be fully collectivised by 1961. The gulf between intention and reality had never been wider. By 1963 the plan had been officially abandoned, with massive shortfalls in key areas. The exodus of key workers prior to the Berlin Wall in 1961 was blamed for the most part, although the genuine reasons (which were partially acknowledged) were failures to assess true capacity and co-ordinate production. The Soviet Union resisted attempts by the SED to revise and re-launch the current plan, with the result that the entire economic system was overhauled to re-emerge as the "New Economic System of Planning and Control" (1963). The new system overcame several weaknesses of previous strategies. Not only were elements of material incentive incorporated for workers and factories (so-called economic "levers"), but planning by setting crude volume target increases gave way to the application of scientific and technical methods to promote genuine progress. Individual plants and factories also received greater freedoms of managerial decision.

Immediately after the failure of the 7-Year Plan the SED announced a "Perspective Plan for 1964-1970", although this did not become law until 1967, so that interim year-plans for 1964, 1965 and 1966 did not form fully part of the longer term strategy. However, the economy stabilised under the influence of the new system and increased growth rates were registered. (The term "perspective plan" was later abandoned in line with Soviet terminology which reserved this for the very long term planning perspectives outlined above).

A third 5-Year Plan for 1966-1970 was notable for not setting rigid production target figures but broad bands. In volume terms the previously stated goal of achieving parity with the FRG was attained at the conclusion of this plan phase.

1967-1970 saw significant alterations made to the New Economic System. While the element of delegation of policy making to the state-owned concerns and regions continued, certain key industries and areas of structural development became subject to separate planning, once again of a more centralist kind. This was termed the "Economic System of Socialism" and was primarily aimed at promoting science and technology in industry, especially in electronics and chemicals and engineering. High investments were approved (180% up on the 1965 levels) and scientific education was accorded priority. The general aim was to enable the GDR to catch up with high technology industries in the west. The strong concentration on "growth" industries, however, was again at the expense of an already weak consumer and distribution sector, with the consequence that poor weather towards the end of 1970 was the catalyst for a severe crisis in the supply of essential goods to the population.

The 5-Year Plan for 1971-1975, although delayed on account of the 1970 crisis, set modest but realistic targets aimed at achieving balanced expansion and rationalisation: in particular production costs were proving excessive, although volume targets in certain areas were being fulfilled. Engineering, electronics and chemicals were selected expansion areas and progress was to be achieved through better managerial techniques, co-operation and specialisation. In comparison with previous plans, industrial investment was curtailed with more attention given to consumer goods and to supplying the needs of the people. In some areas the planned volume targets were exceeded, although work productivity amounted to an annual 5.5% growth as opposed to the intended 6.2%.

Unlike earlier plans, that for 1976-1980 was ready in time and not disrupted through severe shortfalls or crises. It began with target increases of 5% for national income, 7% for industrial production, and 6.5% for worker productivity. These were reduced during the course of the plan but the final achieved average annual increases were 4.1% for national income and 5% for the production of industrial goods (revised target: 6%). Investments rose by 4.8% (target 5.2%) and worker productivity 4.7% (5.4%). Small trade, however, grew by 4.1% (4%) and take-home pay by 3.8% (4%). With an improved consumer sector and social provisions (including a housing programme and higher minimum wages and pensions) the standard of living rose significantly, although luxury goods remained in short supply. After 1973 and the international oil crisis, the GDR ran a trade deficit and accumulated a large national debt - an example of how even planned socialist economies cannot remain immune to world developments.

The 1981-1985 plan tackled the foreign debt problem in two ways. Growth was once again the keyword (national income was to rise annually by between 5.1 and 5.4%), but, this time, financed by exports rather than investment which was earmarked for a modest rise of 1.8 to 2.3%. Private consumption was also scheduled to increase but slightly. The growth industries previously identified continued to enjoy priority, with an emphasis on energy saving measures. Clearly the planners were pursuing their earlier goals of altering the structure of industry through a consistent programme of modernisation and rationalisation. As for agriculture, grain and crop production was to be increased, especially for animal foodstuffs. By 1982 it was evident that the targets were too ambitious, with national income only 3% up in 1982. Although the Soviet Union reduced its oil supplies to the GDR by 10%, exports rose by a huge 14%, albeit at the cost of severe shortages on the home market. At the 11th

SED Party Congress in Berlin 1986, the Party leader, Erich Honecker, reported overall increases in labour productivity, energy saving (down by an annual 5.3%), agricultural output and technological advance in the new industries.

The declared Plan for 1986-1990 continued previous general strategies and adhered to balanced growth, with the needs of the population and consumer and social services not neglected at the expense of industry. Industrial goods turnover is expected to grow at over 5% per year and the production of consumer durables by 30 to 32% in total by 1990: consumer services will rise by over 28% and intensive development in both the co-operative and private crafts sector is promised. The housing shortage will have been resolved, with 1,064,000 more dwellings to be built or modernised. As for crop production, this is intended to rise by an average of 1.7% (livestock: 1.4%). The Soviet Union has also undertaken to continue the supply of raw materials on substantially the same level.

7.4 How Effective are the Plans?

A review of the medium term plans from 1948 until the 1980s reveals that it was not until the late 1960s and early 1970s that the economy was fully stabilised from the post-war situation. An early concentration on basic resources and heavy industry has produced often severe economic discrepancies and consumer sector difficulties which have still not been overcome, despite the re-orientation to different, more modern industries. However, there is no doubt that the planning mechanisms as such are much more sophisticated than in the early years. The conflict between long-term planning and the need to react to immediate crises remains a barrier to the socialist ideal, although the fundamental principles of economic control are still adhered to and are envisaged as offering the best means of providing social and economic stability in the long run.

Finally it must be pointed out that it is not easy to assess the GDR's actual economic performance, largely because of unreliable data, differences in western and socialist methods of computing performance, and the consistent tendency of the GDR's leaders to equate simple growth with progress. The standard measures in the GDR are Produced National Income (PNI) and Industrial Goods Production (IGP), although better indicators are labour productivity, capital productivity and capital intensity. Growth in personal consumption may not, however, progress in line with the economy and the much vaunted stability in the prices of consumer goods can actually conceal a sizeable degree of "hidden" inflation (e.g. in the form of lower quality items sold at the same price).[10]

The problems for the 1980s are not unique to the GDR. The changeover from attempting constant increases in gross productivity to growth in selective "high technology" industries such as microprocessors and robotics is actually a long-term process implying quite considerable social, political and ideological changes that are perhaps little understood, even in the West, with more experience of this recent economic revolution. And despite the GDR's effective "backdoor membership" of the European Community through its links with West Germany,[11] its constant need to import basic materials (30% of domestic needs) as well as to maintain a large land army and armaments programme during a period of political tension between East and West both represent heavy demands on an economy which is, incidentally, also committed to significant improvements in social provision. Whether all of these factors and demands can be met remains to be seen.

CHAPTER 8
EDUCATION IN THE GDR

8.1 Historical Development

After the Second World War the German people were confronted with the material and intellectual ruins that Hitler left behind. There were no proper textbooks except those filled with Nazi ideology and most of the former teachers had been forced to resign because their own ideology and therefore the ideology they spread was fascist. A phase of re-orientation had to begin, new teaching material had to be devised, new textbooks had to be written and new teachers had to be employed. This, of course, was not easy to accomplish as there was a shortage of young, democratic teachers: war and fascism had taken their toll. As a solution to this problem, the so-called Arbeiter- und Bauernfakultäten (Workers' and Farmers' Faculties) were set up, where especially skilled and talented citizens (regardless of their previous profession) underwent a short teacher-training course which enabled them to give lessons to the children of the war. At that time the school system was still the three tier one with Hauptschule, Mittelschule (which gave a qualification comparable to the English O-levels), and Gymnasium or Oberschule (A-levels).

In 1946 the so-called "Antifascist-democratic educational reform" was initiated. This envisaged transforming the old three part structure step by step into a horizontally structured comprehensive school. A little later, in 1952, as part of the new phase into which the East German nation was supposed to be moving, viz. the "Construction of Socialism", the Politbureau passed a resolution intended to raise the level of education and enhance the involvement of the communist party in the general school system. From this moment on the aims of education were inextricably linked to Marxism-Leninism and designed to affirm the leading role of the SED in educational institutions. The theoretical accent was on the general and comprehensive development of the young person's personality, who would thus be able and willing to participate in the establishment of socialism and to understand and enact the esssential "scientific" principles of communism and the means of economic production in a socialist society. The famous "unity of moral and practical education" ("Einheit der Bildung und Erziehung") was enunciated, by which the goals of education may be understood as a harmonious unity, not only between practical and academic knowledge, but also between educational capabilities and socialist awareness.[12] Against the backdrop of these ideas and of Karl Marx's concept of a polytechnical training which would introduce children to the general principles of economic production and the practical tools and instruments of all branches of work,[13] the party began to move towards introducing the so-called "polytechnical" system of school education.

Although the above formulations referred principally to the school system, the universities - criticised by the SED as archaic, reactionary and as bastions of bourgeois opposition - had already been targeted for radical changes. A national secretariat (Staatssekretariat für Hochschulwesen) had been established in 1951 to assume central control of all universities and introduce a unified 10-month year of study with precisely laid down curricula. Marxism and the Russian language became compulsory subjects for all students.

A massive building programme for higher education was also initiated, so that in addition to the existing 6 universities and 15 technical colleges, 25 new institutions were established between 1953 and 1954, many of them devoted to medicine, the practical sciences and economics. From 1951 to 1954 student numbers shot up from 28000 to 57500, with over half coming from working class families. A determined effort was made through positive discrimination to give study places to young working class students at the expense of those from middle class backgrounds.

By the middle 1950s, however, above all in the

humanities, but also in economics, voices began to be raised in the universities expressing opposition to the strict Stalinism of the SED: the basic contradiction between the social utopia as envisaged by Marx and as propagated in the compulsory ideological studies and the reality of SED management served as the main trigger for the resurgence of "revisionism" at this time and the proposal of a "Third Way" to socialism. Several prominent academics entered into direct conflict with the state, e.g. Robert Havemann and Wolfgang Harich, and the philosopher Ernst Bloch left Leipzig for West Germany in 1961 after having had to cease lecturing from 1957. Overall, however, the universal ideological education was producing a class of young graduates at least nonimally grounded in and committed to socialism, even if they were also aware of fundamental contradictions between Marxist theory and its implementation in the contemporary GDR. Many of these graduates, moveover, were fully conscious of the fact that they owed their academic training to the socialist state and that they would not have enjoyed such opportunities in West Germany.

The universities were destined to become "socialist" institutions producing primarily technical specialists with experience in industry and agriculture and a solid background in socialist ideology. The party was making a determined effort not only to catch up with international scientific and research developments but also to create a well educated and loyal class of citizen. Certainly this class grew rapidly in number. In 1958 there existed 46 universities or institutions of higher education and in 1960 228,000 students, which was double those of 1951 and represented about one fifth of the younger generation.[14] The next intitiative in educational policy occurred 1958/1959, when the Central Committee of the SED agreed on further proposals aimed at re-structuring the schools system. These proposals were formally enacted by the People's Chamber in December 1959 and provided for the familiarisation of schoolchildren with industrial production and life at a place of work ("Werkunterricht") as a subject on the curriculum. In addition, there would be greater concentration on science, technical and economic subjects, which would encompass 70% of the total curriculum. Ideological education, of course, was also to be intensified. This structural reform would be completed by 1964 and would see the universal introduction of the "General, Ten-Year Poytechnical Upper School", which would provide standard compulsory education at secondary level throughout the country. Small, single class country schools would close. By 1959 a national school curriculum had been established, which promptly served, however, as a basis for further development in an ongoing attempt to design syllabusses and courses which were not only designed to meet the objective economic and technical demands of a modern industrial state but which also combined academic needs with a concept of personal, "socialist" development. This was perceived as a major and vital task for the future needs of the nation.

8.2 Policy and Aims

In the GDR educational policy is regarded as the most important element of social policy because of its tremendous significance for socialist society in general. Article 17 (2) of the national constitution states that:

> The German Democratic Republic shall assure all citizens a high standard of education corresponding to the constantly increasing social requirements through the integrated socialist education system. It shall enable citizens to shape socialist society and to participate creatively in the development of socialist democracy.[15]

Education in the GDR strives for the development of socialist convictions, socialist character traits and socialist behaviour in an individual. The person who combines all these features is called a "fully-rounded socialist personality". Of course, this implies that education, especially of young people, should always result in an Marxist-Leninist world outlook which should be reflected in their personal beliefs and attitudes. This, the chief aim of education in the GDR, in fact corresponds to Karl Marx's "fully-rounded individual" who "is shaped by means of the harmonious combination$_{16}$ of productive work, instruction and physical training"[16] GDR official policy gives us an idea of what these ideal personalitites could actually be like: they are described as people

> who make full use of their abilities and talents in the best interest of socialist society and who distinguish themselves by the pleasure they gain from work and their readiness to defend their country, by their team spirit and pursuit of great communist ideas.[17]

In order to shape these "fully-rounded socialist personalities" the whole population has to be provided with a high level of education which comprises all major areas of life in nature and society. Each citizen should have a thorough general knowledge and should receive specialised training to a high standard. Pupils should not only understand the developments going on in nature and society, but they should also acquire knowledge in a scientific and practically orientated way - all this, of course, through a proletarian perspective.

The tasks of the educational institutions are described by party officials as follows:

> Our girls and boys are to be well prepared for life, career and participation in society, not only to be good skilled workers, but also to play their full part later on as conscious, intelligent and active citizens. On the one hand, this makes it necessary to give all children an equally high, thorough and scientifically based general education. Social sciences, arts, language and natural sciences instruction are, therefore, on a par with poytechnical education and physical training. On the other hand, they are educated to think and act creatively and they are offered many opportunities for developing their special inclinations and aptitudes.[18]

The most important practical element of socialist general knowledge is the "polytechnische Erziehung" (technological training). This is to prepare children and young people for the world of work and production, for technology and the economy, ensuring that they acquire the qualifications and expertise which enable them to be creative citizens who actively take part in planning, administration and in government affairs.

8.3 The Education Act of 1965

1965 was a milestone in the long process of educational reform initiated by the SED. The People's Chamber passed a law enacting the "unified socialist education system" and at last fulfilling the 1959 proposals for the ten-year polytechnical school. The law encompassed the entire educational system of the GDR, from school to tertiary level, and included provision for adult and vocational training. Although the 1965 measures determined the basic structures and features of education as it exists today, provision for continuing reform was already incorporated. Within the general framework of a precisely laid down and controlled school curriculum, which had been established for the first time in 1959, Marxism-Leninism was expanded as a compulsory subject for schoolchildren. Under Honecker, the role of ideology in school education has, if anything, increased even further and was re-affirmed at the Party Congresses of 1971, 1976 and 1981. As far as implementation of reform policy is concerned, the process of designing and preparing the necessary aims, content and pratical course materials - not to mention provision for in-service teacher training - for the new national curricula has required a mammoth effort on the part of educationalists which has extended into the 1970s and beyond. Predictably, those subjects such as history and civic studies have required more frequent ideological revision than other, politically less sensitive areas. An important issue of the 1970s has been the tension between the pedagogic need for educational flexibility alongside continual revision of the curriculum and the rigidity implicit in a fixed, long-term national syllabus. Whereas educationalists have tended to stress the former, politicians have regarded stability and uniformity as the essential keystones of the system.[19] The immediate fruits of the new school education included a rapid extension of educational opportunities for children. If, in 1951, only 16% of children stayed at school for more than eight years, this rose to 65% in 1960 and 72% in 1966. Sport, of course, was intensively promoted in the schools, with many national sporting occasions and festivals being staged for workers and the general public as well as for young people. At international level, of course, this most determined investment in sport resulted in the GDR achieving third place behind the USA and the USSR in the 1968 Mexico Olympics.

8.4 Career Selection

Sport aside, however, the educational system of the GDR is generally acknowledged to be far superior to that of West Germany, especially in terms of opportunities offered. Moreover, a real effort is made to co-ordinate intellectual capabilities with academic training and to provide the best possible match of personal interests with career selection. To this end, schoolchildren from a relatively early age participate in a programme of vocational familiarisation and orientation ("Berufsaufklärung" or "Berufsorientierung") which gives first hand experience of the world of work and is intended to engender positive attitudes towards important areas of economic and industrial activity. In the light of the economic plan, it is ascertained just what future careers are likely to be available for current twelve year-olds, who, when the time comes to leave school, should be in a position to apply on an individual and completely voluntary basis for a job or apprenticeship in a particular field. School and industry work together in this process to ensure as far as possible that vacancies match demand. Despite the care and attention that this system implies, however, several problems do arise. Firstly, it has not often not been possible to match the preferred careers with what is actually on offer, and, secondly, the long-term approach to vocational guidance fails when those priority careers to which schoolchildren are being directed abruptly disappear through economic or political factors. Lastly, personal connections can count for more than the objective system of guidance and selection, especially where prestige or otherwise attractive jobs are involved: naturally this produces a sense of unfairness and resentment.

8.5 Education and the State

As in all other communist states there is in principle no private education sector in the GDR. On the one hand this means that there are neither private schools nor private publishers of textbooks, on the other hand there is the advantage that no school or university fees etc. have to be paid. All educational facilities, including coaching at school, are free of charge, and nobody is allowed to make profits from education.

The strict division between Church and State in the GDR gives rise to another aspect of educational policy, viz. secular education. Officially the Church has no influence at all on education, and members of the Church are therefore only allowed to hold their religious classes on their own premises and in their own time.

As noted above, education in the GDR is of fundamental importance for the overall development of socialist society and so all educational facilities and institutions - from the creche to university - are naturally brought under state control. The entire educational system is fully controlled by the Ministerium für Volksbildung (Ministry of Education), which plans and co-ordinates education: it sets strict regulations governing curricula, school rules, the training of teachers, etc. It also plans education in accordance with the economic requirements of the GDR. Moreover, the Ministry of Education sets a minimum standard for school facilities and it provides all the funds required.

Finally it is worth mentioning that the family as such is, of course, regarded as an important educational "institution" as well, and "co-operation and participation in decision-making at school"[20] is encouraged by the authorities.

The constitution of the GDR guarantees each citizen "an equal right to education" (Article 25 (1)) and it furthermore states that:

... educational facilities shall be open to all. The integrated socialist education system shall guarantee every citizen a continuous socialist education, training and further training.[21]

But the constitution not only guarantees certain rights to its citizens; it is also regarded as every citizen's <u>duty</u> to learn a trade or profession and to take advantage of the many opportunities offered for further education, as, for example, in extra-mural courses or evening classes:

.... and to acquire new knowledge throughout their lives, to keep up-to-date and be well prepared for the new tasks set by scientific and technological advance.[22]

The guarantee of an equal right to education for all is reflected in the fact that all pupils actually receive the same education throughout the country - irrespective of where they live or what their social background is. To make sure that all pupils receive equal education (and nobody is given preference), the same textbooks are used nationwide and the curricula are the same everywhere. But, most important of all, there is only one kind of schooling available throughout the country: it is an integrated school which is attended by all children for ten years, the <u>Allgemeinbildende</u> <u>Polytechnische</u> <u>Oberschule</u> (comprehensive polytechnical school). Despite its uniformity, however, education is valued extremely highly and it plays an essential role in the process of social advancement.

8.6 Pre-School Education

If required, the state takes care of children from birth onwards. Attendance at the two pre-school institutions, Kinderkrippe (creche) and Kindergarten (nursery school), is not compulsory, but nevertheless around 60% of children up to three years of age are looked after in a creche and around 90% of three to six year olds attend nursery schools. The reason the latter figure is so high can be explained by the fact that in most families both parents are working. As so many mothers do shiftwork, the Kindergarten is open from 6 a.m to 7 p.m.

Because all education is under state control, activities and timetables in creches and nursery schools are organised and planned by state authorities. Some of the activities in this so-called "first stage of the integrated socialist education system" include physical training (i.e. dancing and gymnastics), the development of hygiene habits, the instilling of orderliness, games, roleplaying, language development and art work. There are also a few nursery schools run by the Church. These are not, however, officially recognised as pre-school institutions.

Prior to entering compulsory school education particular efforts are made to prepare both children and parents for the changeover. This also affects children who have not attended nursery, for whom a programme of special afternoon sessions devoted to "play and learning" is laid on.

8.7 The Ten-Year General Polytechnical Upper School

With this cumbersome title is implied a basic ("general") secondary education lasting for ten school years and combining academic skills with a familiarity with the world of work in a technologically productive socialist society (i.e. it is "polytechnical" in orientation). The term "Upper School" is an indication not just of standards but also of the intention to lay a foundation for extended or vocational education. The detailed curriculum for all subjects is laid down nationally with books and course materials either produced or approved by the Ministry of Education.

There are three stages or levels in the polytechnical school. The Lower Stage comprises classes (= years) 1 to 3 (ages 7 to 9), the Middle Stage classes 4 to 6 (ages 10 to 12), and the Upper Stage classes 7 to 10 (ages 13 to 17).

At the Lower or Primary Stage the child is helped to understand his environment and acquainted with primary study skills. The most striking feature in the primary stage of education is the dominance of German as a subject (mainly language and literature, but also a little East German geography). This is designed to strengthen reading and writing skills quite early. Another reason for the significance of this subject is that in dealing with literature pupils are exposed to certain patterns of (socialist) behaviour, character traits and attitudes which are helpful for the overall development of the "fully-rounded socialist personality". After German the second principal subject is mathematics. Teaching methods and course materials in both of these areas are traditional by western standards (e.g. mathematical set theory plays no part and standards of neatness in handwriting are important). The polytechnical component is already introduced in the subject "Werkunterricht" (translatable, perhaps, as "industrial arts") and as a component of German studies, which is also designed to inform the children about their own country. The first step towards developing practical skills is taken with weekly lessons in gardening (in the school garden) and in "Werkunterricht".

The Middle Stage sees the introduction of Russian, history, geography, physics and biology and, usually after completion of the first year of this stage (class 4), the chance to enter specialist classes or even schools offering increased facilities for the especially gifted (e.g. in sport, music, languages, mathematics and the sciences). Planning and guidance for a child's working career also begins during this stage.

The Upper or Senior Stage is divided into two stages. The first, classes 7 and 8, completes the period of basic compulsory and unified schooling (the Einheitsschule), after which the children will embark on qualitatively different paths of education or training depending on their interests and aptitudes. From class 7, too, English or French is offered as a second optional language, and pupils gain practical experience of work in industry and in agriculture: this work experience and participation in actual production is linked to the subject of "polytechnical education" which is an essential part of the curriculum.

Most schoolchildren in the GDR go on to the second level of the Upper Stage, classes 9 and 10. Pupils who leave after the 8th class at the age of fifteen enter trades or other vocations to become trainees or apprentices, during which period they also continue with their further general school education.

8.8 Military Education

A, from an international point of view, unique element of the GDR's educational programme is the so-called "sozialistische Wehrerziehung" (socialist military education) which primarily concerns senior pupils. The aims of this military education are, among others, to develop a readiness to defend the country (and socialism) by military force, to consolidate socialist patriotism and the achievements of socialism in general. Military education is already part of the activities within the youth organisations, Junge Pioniere and Freie Deutsche Jugend as well as the para-military Gesellschaft für Sport und Technik, and it is regarded as most important at the Polytechnische Oberschule, where the "subject", "Wehrerziehung", was made compulsory in 1978 for all pupils of both sexes in the 9th and 10th classes. In both these years the subject is taught in four double lessons, and in addition, pupils in the 9th year have either to take part in a special twelve day course in a military camp where they receive practical instruction from officers and soldiers of the Nationale Volksarmee (National People's Army). Compulsory reading for all pupils is the 350 page reference manual, Wissensspeicher Wehrunterricht, which covers topics from military games and acquiring observation techniques to an introduction to arms and weapons systems. Furthermore, a special chapter describes how to use a handgun. The instructions given here can be put into practice in a special room for target practice, which headmasters at Polytechnische Oberschulen are bound to provide. Training in physical fitness and technical subjects (e.g. radio communications, driving, seamanship) is given, effectively as a kind of preparation for national service.

On conclusion of the 10th class pupils - including those who left full-time education after the eighth class - sit a written final school-leaving examination in German, maths, Russian, and a science such as physics, chemistry or biology. To this examination also belong oral tests in two optional subjects and in sport. The result is an overall single assessment on a five point scale ranging from very good to unsatisfactory, with special provision for exceptionally good performance.

8.9 The Extended Upper School

Qualifications for further education and university entrance (Abitur) can be acquired in the so-called "Extended Upper School" (Erweiterte Oberschule or EOS). This consists of two further school years (classes 11 and 12), during which pupils are taught according to a general foundation curriculum for university study. The certificate thus gained entitles the pupil only to apply for a place at university, not necessarily in the subject of his choice (it does not guarantee acceptance): study places are in fact subject to a strict selection process which often begins in the 10th class. Since 1981 the number of separate EOS institutions has dropped in favour of a system in which the EOS forms an adjunct to the general polytechnical school itself.

Compulsory subjects at the EOS comprise German, Russian, maths and a second foreign language, alongside physics, chemistry, biology, geography, history, civic studies and sport. The pupil must further choose between art studies or music and has the chance of a wide programme of options under the heading of "scientific practical work" - an extension of the polytechnical studies described above. The final examination comprises both written and oral parts and is awarded with a single overall assessment mark. By this time the school leaver will have reached the age of 18.

For those who left full-time education earlier, say at the end of the 10th class, at the age of 16, provision is available for attaining the general Abitur in two years at special courses organised at people's higher educational institutions (Volkshochschulen): main subjects here include German, maths, physics, chemistry and civic or ideological studies (Staatsbürgerkunde). Alongside this, a more specialised Abitur can be done in three years which is designed to prepare candidates for entry into technical and engineering studies or economics and subsequent careers.

The selection of school pupils for the EOS itself is highly competitive. Local school commissions are formed to assess the candidate's academic performance as well as his wider social behaviour, his commitment to the GDR, and his economic background (working class children are favoured). Similarly, for younger people at work or older citizens admitted to the special two or three year Abitur courses, the selection process involves social assessment and the views of the factory or place of work (with positive discrimination in favour of girls/women).

In the light of an increasing trend towards a workforce which is technically overqualified in relation to the jobs actually performed, the state has made a determined effort to reduce the number of schoolchildren and others doing the Abitur and hence being able to proceed to higher education (especially noticeable since the 8th SED Party Congress of 1971). Thus in 1982 only 10% of pupils in the 10th class progressed to the EOS and 5% of those at work were admitted to Abitur courses. The most recent national priorities, formulated at SED congresses in the 1970s onwards, value the need for more highly qualified artisans above academic training, with the result that access to university has been restricted. In this sense, it is questionable whether the GDR genuinely provides every citizen with access to the highest forms of education appropriate to his abilities. The selective admission to Abitur courses, is, of course, in itself a discrete method of reducing the student population and hence the scale of participation in further academic education. State officials admit

> ... that there cannot be unlimited access to colleges and universities as well as to Abitur classes and technical schools. The demand for highly qualified personnel in all sectors is established on a long-term basis and the number of students at universities, colleges and technical schools is planned accordingly for the different disciplines.[23]

8.10 Polytechnical Education in more Detail

Polytechnical education can simply be defined as a combination of traditional lessons with work. This unique kind of education, which became compulsory in the GDR in 1959, is officially described as follows:

> (It) involves the acquisition of technological and economic knowledge, practical work skills and an insight into productive work[24]

In short, it aims to prepare young people for work, technology and production. Moreover, it is expected that the pupils will develop respect for work in general as well as for working people. By means of polytechnical education young people are furthermore to gain an insight into how workers "have a say at their workplace" and to learn about the significance work has for socialist society.

And, last but not least, it is claimed that through polytechnical education pupils have the chance to make contacts with workers in the working conditions of the enterprise. As is shown in figure 4, 10.6% of the curriculum involves polytechnical training. In comparison to figures like 41.4% of the curriculum consisting of social sciences, arts and music, or 29.8% maths and natural sciences, the percentage for polytechnical education seems rather low. It is worth remembering, however, that polytechnical education is not restricted to the special polytechnical subjects. Most other school subjects like maths, natural sciences, or even German (it should not be forgotten, for example, that literature is significant for shaping certain character traits, etc.) contribute to polytechnical education by giving the pupils insights into technology, sciences and so on.

From the first year to the sixth year both boys and girls are taught in special school workshops where, by doing woodwork and gardening in the school garden, they acquire first theoretical knowledge and practical work-skills at an early age.

Starting from the seventh year the pupils receive polytechnical instruction once a week by taking part in the actual work processes in an enterprise for two to three hours per week. (the enterprise could be a state-owned farm or factory). This part of the polytechnical education is called "Introduction to Socialist Production".

In the Integrated Socialist Education System Act of 1965 nationally-owned enterprises are actually bound to meet both material and personnel requirements for polytechnical education. For this reason polytechnical centres, production departments or polytechnical laboratories are found in most enterprises, where the pupils are taught either by specially trained teachers or by suitably skilled workers.

It is stressed by party officials that this kind of education fulfills its function of preparing young people for their future jobs and of helping them to find out by instruction or guidance which profession they would like to follow later in life. Although the essence of this statement is applicable in most cases, there have been reports which imply quite the contrary (there was one case where pupils had to fold flour sacks day after day, or had to sort out hundreds of nails and screws). It sometimes seems difficult for management to provide sensible and useful fields of activity in which pupils might gain the insights and experiences mentioned above.

8.11 Special Schools

The term "special schools" (Spezialschulen) here will be taken to mean special educational provision for the gifted. This is somewhat at variance with usage in the UK, where "special education" commonly refers to facilities for handicapped children (Sonderschulen in German). About 2.8% of the annual school population of the GDR attend a variety of schools for the handicapped, depending on the individual's age, disability and educational capabilities.

At various stages from class 3 upwards, particularly gifted children in the unified polytechnical school can be directed towards special classes or separate schools which enjoy enhanced facilities for developing exceptional aptitudes, primarily in foreign languages (especially Russian, which is the most commonly taken up of the specialist subjects and draws its entrants from class 3 onwards), maths and sciences, music and sport (promising gymnasts start special training from the age of five or six). Special classes exist within the Polytechnische Oberschule for subjects which can be taught within the overall curriculum, such as foreign languages or mathematics, while special schools exist for those subjects which cannot be easily integrated into the normal curriculum and school environment, such as music and sports. Staff-pupil ratio is high in these special classes and the timetable devotes more time than normal to the subject at which the child excels. An increase of provision for foreign languages and the sciences reflects current priorities in international affairs and industry, although the special schools as such are not given a high public profile since their inescapably elitist nature runs against the grain of the unified comprehensive system. Competition to enter the special classes or schools is, however, very stiff, as they take up only 3% of schoolchildren but virtually guarantee university entrance. Despite the nominal applicability of the normal criteria for entrance, it helps a lot if the parents are highly placed in the SED and the state apparatus!

Despite a widely acknowledged superiority to its West German counterpart (which has remained on a very conservative level since 1945), the school system of the GDR has not necessarily remained true to its own propagated base of equality. From the 8th class onwards (14th year), the marked differentiation of opportunity and the creation of academic elites comprising statistically very small minorities within the general school population undoubtedly undermines the ideological claim that the system is unified, comprehensive, and offers truly equal opportunities. Indeed, the appearance of parallel, vertical educational paths at the top end of the Upper School which are to all intents and purposes impossible to cross characterises those very historical features of school systems in capitalist countries that the GDR has claimed to overcome.

8.12 Vocational Training

Aside from the school system, there exists comprehensive provision for vocational training for schoolleavers (especially the minority who leave school at 14 or 16 after only eight years at school). This may last between one and four years, depending on age, school qualification and the vocation itself, and combines theoretical and practical training in officially designated careers. The training invariably takes place in something akin to a local British Technical College orientated towards vocational courses (Berufsschulen). Of particular importance are currently 28 designated "basic vocations" which are held to be of especial value to the economy and range from engineering and computers to skills in agriculture and finance.

To summarise, school pupils in the GDR have three possible ways of taking their Abitur: first, by attending the Erweiterte Oberschule which directly adjoins the Polytechnische Oberschule and leads to study at university. This school, where advanced level studies are undertaken, can only be attended by a certain percentage of pupils each year who are especially gifted or talented. The second possibility is by doing a three-year vocational training course combined with Abitur, and the third possible way is via adult education in evening classes or at special academies.

While a small percentage of pupils start with a three-year vocational training course after only eight years at school, the majority of schoolchildren in the GDR attend the Polytechnische Oberschule for ten years before starting either a two-year vocational course or a three-year vocational course which includes the Abitur.

A high proportion of mature citizens and workers partake in an ongoing programme of general and further education which is centred on the so-called Betriebsschulen or Betriebsakademien (= schools and academies related to factories and places of work). These institutions concentrate on professional and work-related training (e.g. to the level of master, or "Meister", of a trade within about two years), whereas the Volkshochschulen (People's Colleges of Higher Education) enable working people to update their general level of formal education to that of the 10th or 12th class of the Upper School. Currently the GDR is doing a great deal to help girls and women attain technical qualifications at their place of work (only one third of women in industrial production are qualified skilled workers) by means of financial assistance, free time and special help for mothers. In view of the reduction in opportunities for university education for academically qualified schoolleavers of the EOS, these are now directed towards eighteen-month long courses which will enable them to become qualified skilled workers in an area corresponding to that which they wanted to study at university.

In order to fulfil the guarantee of equal opportunity of education for all and to enable every citizen with certain interests and talents to enter the next stage in the education system, one very important principle established by the state is the interchangeability of the elements of the education programme. Although there are aspects in the GDR's educational policy which can be criticized, the remarkable number of citizens doing adult education seems to prove that this aspect of the system is working and fulfilling its promises in most cases. In 1977 alone 1,455,300 adults attended academies or took part in higher education courses, 573,000 of whom were females!

8.13 Outside School Hours

Despite differences in scale and orientation much of the above system of school and further education corresponds in basic provision and intention to that available in western countries. However, a major aim of the socialist system is to extend institutionalised socialist education to the whole of the child's day, including his leisure hours. "Whole-Day-Schools" (Ganztagsschulen) embodying this goal, however, have not yet been introduced in large measure, possibly because of economic considerations. Meanwhile, for younger schoolchildren, so-called School Nurseries (Schulhorte), which are integrated into the school itself, and Children's Nurseries (Kinderhorte), which are independant of a particular school, provide care and activities outside actual school hours. The programme of such nurseries is carefully directed by trained personnel, and includes homework, educational play, instruction in social behaviour and ideology, scientific activities and sport and recreation.

Older children (aged 15 to 16) may participate in "Extra-Curricular Work-Groups" (Außerunterrichtliche Arbeitsgemeinschaften) which complement school studies

The Education System of the GDR

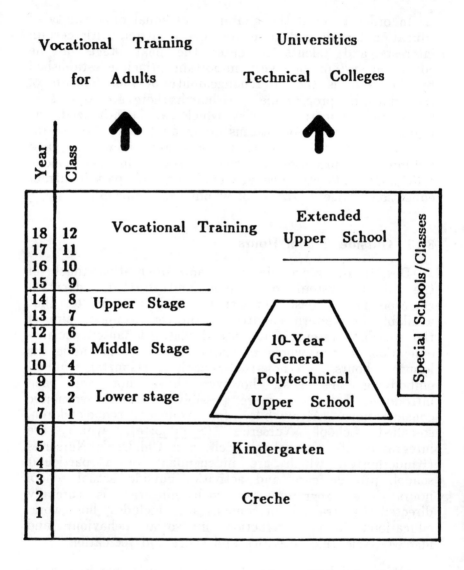

Vocational   Training

for   Adults

Universities

Technical   Colleges

Year	Class			
18	12	Vocational Training	Extended	
17	11		Upper School	
16	10			
15	9			
14	8	Upper Stage		
13	7			
12	6	Middle Stage	10-Year General Polytechnical Upper School	
11	5			
10	4			
9	3	Lower stage		
8	2			
7	1			
6		Kindergarten		
5				
4				
3		Creche		
2				
1				

Special Schools/Classes

and promote artistic and cultural interests according to precisely laid down programmes.

A very important element in the education system of the GDR is taken up by the youth organisations Ernst Thälmann Junge Pioniere (= JP; for children between 6 and 14 years of age) and especially the Freie Deutsche Jugend (FDJ; for young people from 14 years of age). Membership of these organisations is not compulsory, but nevertheless around 75% of all children and young people have joined either the JP or FDJ. There are no official figures as to how many actually join these organizations only so as not to be excluded from social life and possibly from promotion later on, but it is known that life can become rather complicated and difficult if you are not in one of the youth organizations.

The role of both these organizations in the educational system should not be underestimated. The JP are said to contribute to education by offering a versatile and interesting life in the collective. They have actually set up 110,100 study groups in schools (arranging spare-time events in the collective) and they run 6,000 choirs throughout the country. Today, around 1.6 million pupils between six and fourteen years take part in spare-time group activities organized by the JP, which has its own libraries, theatres and sporting facilities, usually in "Young Pioneer Houses" and "Pioneer Parks" throughout the country.

The FDJ can be regarded as one of the most important social sub-systems in the GDR. Very early in the GDR's history it accepted the communist party's leading role in politics and followed the aims set up by the party. Around 75% of the 14 to 25 year-old age group are members of the FDJ (in 1981 the FDJ had 2.3 million members). The chief aim of the organization is to educate the growing generation to be class-conscious socialists who work, live and learn the socialist way. The FDJ provides extra-curricular activities for this age group. Like the JP it mainly works directly in the schools, where FDJ groups organize and control a wide variety of activities, from the annual Maths Olympics to political projects and rallies and to coaching at school. However, it is important to note that FDJ officials may attend exams and interviews and that they may deal with problems arising at school. More importantly, their committees even, as is stated in the 1974 Youth Act of the GDR, "shall have the right to a say in the decision on admission" to university.

Although the youth organizations are not, then, an official part of the school curriculum, they play an important part in an individual's educational progress.

Finally, although the GDR acknowledges the family as an essential cell of human socialisation and upbringing, it is obvious from such a large and resourceful apparatus that as much as possible in the way of the values of socialism is transmitted through formal and organised institutions, so that the chances of the child acquiring anti-communist attitudes through the less easily controllable unit of the family is minimised.

8.14 An Assessment of the Education System

A final assessment of the GDR's educational system might conclude that it is efficient and appropriate to the needs of the nation. Highly positive aspects are the resourcing of facilities and equality of opportunity, despite the marked reduction of higher education places which set in from 1971 and unmistakable features of elitism, especially at the upper end of the secondary school. In terms of pre-school education and staff-pupil ratios, the GDR is now almost certainly well in advance of, say, the British school system, which has experienced severe underfunding and demoralisation during the 1980s. The number of schoolchildren in the GDR entering the sixth form to acquire qualifications for university entrance is not very different from, say, in West Germany, and it is clearly the state's intention to direct children towards practical and technical contrast.

A particular problem when looking at the GDR is how to gain a clear picture of actual school life and teaching practice. Weighing up journalists' observations (some time ago a West German TV team was even allowed to film a school lesson in the GDR) and the comments of GDR citizens, it is possible to say that the level of education in the GDR is very high, and, as far as the imparting of knowledge is concerned, the GDR has nothing to fear from any comparison with western countries. The potential aspects, in particular, of close links between lessons and work experience are also appreciated in western states. Indeed, some West German schools have introduced a similar programme for pupils in their final years at school.

The price for the high level of education in the GDR's schools is an equally high stress on achievement-orientation and an (almost military) discipline. Classes are, moreover, highly teacher-centred: teacher-directed activity seems to dominate in the classroom and active involvement in the shaping of lessons and school affairs generally is not encouraged. The type of teaching which responds to pupils and their interests does not seem to be part of everyday school life in the GDR. Political opponents in the GDR have raised the question whether such teaching practices can effectively lead to creativity, activity and the development of democratic behaviour. In their opinion the educational policy takes away the pupils' ability to decide for themselves and this leads to acceptance, apathy and resignation, or, recently in some cases, to a drop-out mentality. Community activities (within the FDJ or other organizations) which the pupils have to show they have taken part in when they want to apply for a place at an institution of higher education or for a job, are often regarded only as necessary steps to promote a career. There is no doubt that these subjective observations are in sharp contrast to the educational ideals and the aim of the "fully rounded socialist personality". If the authorities in the GDR are serious about their educational aims, they need to carry out basic reforms within the centralized educational system and in particular in classroom teaching practice in order to give the pupils a realistic say in society. The inevitable conclusion is that this is not really wanted at the moment in the GDR. A recent party conference has made clear that the leadership of the communist party wants to promote more creativity in production and the economy in general while Erich Honecker himself has pointed out that the ability to learn and work independantly should be given more encouragement.

CHAPTER 9
CULTURAL POLICY

9.1 The Early Years

As early as 1950 the SED began to state its views on art and culture and to indicate what would and would not be acceptable in the new republic. From the beginning it rejected modern art as formalistic and anti-socialist and advocated the approach of "social realism", which was also promoted in the film industry. The historical "humanistic tradition" of German culture was also deliberately upheld in the performance or publication of the works of Beethoven, Herder and Schiller - especially, as in the case of Schiller, where the themes reflected social justice and the struggle against feudal tyranny.

As for literature, the intitial policy was to admit a wide range of authors and poets as long as they had been banned under Hitler. Hence there appeared, apart from a number of Soviet writers and German pro-communists like Anna Seghers, Johannes R. Becher, Erich Weinert, Willi Bredel, Egon Kisch and Bertolt Brecht, the works of the pacifist Arnold Zweig and of the social critic of the bourgeoisie, Heinrich Mann. The dominant theme of the socialist writers in this early period is that of reconstruction, and this persisted until the beginning of the 1960s. An extreme example is Hans Marchwitza's novel, Pig Iron (Roheisen, 1955) which, in its altruistic depiction of the heroic deeds of workers fulfilling production requirements, even attracted some derision from contemporary East German critics. More sophisticated examples of the literature of reconstruction appear in the early work of Eduard Claudius, who, in his short story, "A Difficult Beginning" (Vom schweren Anfang, 1950) and novel, People at our Side (Menschen an unserer Seite, 1951), describes the problems of life and work in the Soviet Zone and the newly founded Republic. Not until the 1960s, however, did the generally didactic and apologistic approach, with its simplified views of right and wrong, of socialist good and anti-communist evil, give way to a more differentiated consideration of social problems and of conflicts within the GDR which included those of individuals of bourgeois origin attempting to come to grips with the demands of a society orientated towards material production (the so-called "literature of arrival").

By about 1953 the SED was taking a keen interest in the direction of cultural matters and there was a member of the Central Committee - Paul Wandel - responsible for culture in the GDR, which was considered subject to political party policy along with all other aspects of society and life.

At its 5th Party Congress in 1958 the SED announced a major new ideological intitiative to capture the minds of the populace now that the basic material preconditions for the establishment of the post-war socialist state had been set (in the form of the nationalisation of industry and progress in the collectivisation of agriculture). In the words of Ulbricht at the Congress, the keynotes of this initiative were "formation of socialist consciousness", the transmission of the "scientific world view" of Marxism-Leninism, and "socialist ethics and morality". What this meant for the worker was a commitment to meeting productivity targets (the "socialist work ethic") and being enabled - through the role of culture - to develop into an educated, knowledgeable personality possessing a variety of interests and participating actively in society. Shortly before this Congress the SED had deliberated in some depth on the cultural issue and expressed concern at the gap between art and life, which it was up to socialist practioners of art to overcome; there was a pressing need for a truly "socialist German culture"[25] which would counteract and replace the decadent cultural influences from the West that were being uncritically absorbed in the GDR.

9.2 The Bitterfeld Way and Social Realism

The outcome of the SED's cultural initiative was the First Cultural Conference of Writers in the industrial town of Bitterfeld on the 24th April 1959. Here was coined the famous slogan "Reach for your pen, fellow worker. The socialist German national culture needs you!" ("Greif zur Feder, Kumpel. Die sozialistische deutsche Nationalkultur braucht Dich!") which epitomized the so-called "Bitterfeld Way" (Bitterfelder Weg), that is, the new policy of encouraging ordinary workers to take up writing (or painting) in order to discover and promote fresh and genuinely "socialist" artistic talents. "Workers' Writing Circles" (Zirkel schreibender Arbeiter) were set up nationally in the larger factories, clubs and communities and the most talented individuals to emerge from these were organised into "Working Communities of Young Authors" (Arbeitsgemeinschaften junger Autoren or AJA). Often, however, such circles became a refuge, not for artistically minded workers, but for students, officials, journalists, even housewives of limited literary capabilities.[26] The sole approved style, of course, was that of social realism, which was conceived to represent on the cultural level the revolutionary objectives and principles of Marxism-Leninism through giving voice to the ideas and needs of the working masses. Social realism is, then, the cultural expression of the working class, of its historical struggles and its breakthrough to socialism. As a result the principle theme of social realism is to be found in the lives and problems of the ordinary working class, especially in situations of conflict with capitalism, and in the depiction of the worker-revolutionary as a heroic figure. A realistic, non-abstract and authentic descriptive style is cultivated and "partiality" or, in other words, approval of and commitment to the workers' cause, must be evident. The life and vitality of the working class are key elements in the aesthetic of social realism, which is, moreover, international in character (i.e. informed by Soviet art and literature) and not restricted to any particular genre or art form. Social realism was held to set unique and previously unachieved standards in artistic expression and considered inherently superior in its aesthetics and

morality to the art of the West. The human being found
his ultimate expression as the true subject of history and
in the depiction of the laws of social evolution conquering
injustice, poverty and exploitation.

During the late 1950s and early 1960s many East
German writers and poets gained an international
reputation. Bruno APITZ published in 1958 Naked among
Wolves (Nackt unter Wölfen), which depicts how a
resistance group inside Buchenwald concentration camp
risks its own existence in rescuing a Polish child (Apitz
himself was imprisoned for eight years in Buchenwald). In
1960 appeared Dieter NOLL's The Adventures of Werner
Holt. A Novel about Youth (Die Abenteuer des Werner
Holt. Roman einer Jugend), which protrays the history of
a generation which evolves from connivance with fasicism
under Hitler to a position of critical self-analysis - an
instance of the so-called "transformation novel"
(Wandlungsroman) which was popular in both the FRG
and the GDR for Germans attempting to come to grips
with their past. This novel enjoyed a phenomenal success
in the GDR, with a circulation of over 1.5 million,
received national honours and was also filmed. A sequel,
however, Werner Holt. Novel about a Return (Werner
Holt. Roman einer Heimkehr) was not as successful in
that it concentrated less on the work's post-war scenario
than upon the hero's personal search for a woman. Both
Apitz and Noll were communists before the war and
remained committed to socialism within the GDR.

Another novel of this period, Description of a Summer
(Beschreibung eines Sommers) by Karl-Heinz JAKOBS,
which appeared 1961, is an example of the ethos of
Bitterfeld in dealing with the problems and soul-searching
of a non-political engineer at a period when the
communist party is trying to increase the socialist
consciousness of the individual. Jakobs moved to West
Germany in 1981. A further novelist, Uwe JOHNSON,
provoked immediate critical interest with his Speculations
about Jakob (Mutmassungen über Jakob), but emigrated
promptly to the West after its publication in 1959. This
work uses unconventional linguistic and narrative

techniques to depict various (occasionally contradictory) recollections about the death of a railway worker, leaving it to the reader to decide what is the truth and also which of the two Germanies is the superior to live in. In subsequent works Johnson takes up the theme of the division of Germany and is by no means uncritical of conditions in either. In an early novel, The Boys who are Left (Die Jungen, die übrig bleiben - 1950), the writer Erich LOEST depicts the rather tentative gropings of a generation towards a new beginning during the final phase of the war and the occupation. Loest was imprisoned from 1957 till 1964 for "counter-revolutionary activities" and moved to West Germany in 1981.

One of the most important influences on the younger generation of East German writers has been the author and poet Johannes BOBROWSKI, for whom a recurring theme is the guilt-ridden relationship of the German people to their eastern neighbours: the depiction of this historical relationship and the clash of nationalist and social tensions which it has produced is viewed by Bobrowski as a contribution to the effort to counteract modern "revanchist" tendencies. Published work includes the the poetry anthologies, Sarmation Time (Sarmatische Zeit, 1961) and Shadow Land Rivers (Schattenland Ströme, 1962), and the novels Levin's Mill (Levins Mühle, 1964) and Lithuanian Pianos (Litauische Klaviere, 1966).

9.3 Theatre, Music, Opera, Film

The same commitment to a specifically socialist orientation as was being promoted in literature was similarly aimed for by the SED in other areas of artistic activity.

In the theatre this meant that progressive non-communist works could be performed as well as the standard world classics. In the musical field the need for more contemporary composers to create a "socialist musical culture"[27] was acknowledged, and composers such as Wagner and Strauss, who had been popular under

Hitler, were to be performed less often.

The film industry, of course, offered a potentially powerful medium for the GDR's cultural propagandists. In 1958 the national film making organisation, DEFA (Deutsche-Film-AG), was enjoined to create a "socialist cinema" through the appropriate theme of the revolutionary class struggle in Germany. The role of the woman as a worker and working class youth in the GDR were also to be highlighted. From 1959 to 1960 the organisation produced 55 non-documentary films for cinema and also a number of television films.[28] In general, the SED was concerned to give all major cultural activities a didactic socialist purpose, although this educative process did not, for example, preclude in itself the production by DEFA of humourous items for popular entertainment. However, the enduring attraction of light entertainment from the West, especially pop culture appealing to young people, invoked the particular disapproval of the SED and the party made determined efforts to discourage its consumption. Performance fees which had to be paid in hard western currency to foreign agencies further led the authorities to attempt to reduce the population's interest in this area of "subversive" culture.

In 1960 the Politbureau of the Central Committee set up a special commission to control and harmonise issues of both ideology and culture. This commission submitted and implemented directives in these areas and also promoted the teaching of Marxism-Leninism within the internal education system of the SED itself.[29]

9.4 1965: An Ideological Winter

Two years after the proclamation of the New Economic System at the 6th Party Congress of 1963, which had produced a certain liberalisation in economic planning, the course was hardened again with signs of a return to more centralised control (Ulbricht announced a "Second Stage" in the NES).

From 1963 up to this moment the SED had tolerated a degree of constructive social and cultural criticism in literature in keeping with the Bitterfeld conference. Thus Christa WOLF's The Divided Sky (Der geteilte Himmel, 1963, film version 1967), one of the most successful and popular novels in the GDR, was written almost entirely within the spirit of the Bitterfeld programme insamuch as it analyses the relationship of a highly intelligent young scientist of difficult and egoistic social temperament with that of a student teacher of straightforward village origins who ultimately experiences the prospect of integration into the caring socialist community after the liasion collapses. With an academic background in German literature and editor of the leading East German literary journal New German Literature (Neue Deutsche Literatur), Christa Wolf was for a while a member of the Central Committee of the SED, until, however, she failed to be re-elected at the 7th Party Congress of 1967 - a tangible demotion in East German terms and presumably caused by her lack of commitment to the dogmatic line adopted after 1965.

In The Auditorium (Die Aula, 1965), Hermann KANT takes as his theme the development of the Peasants and Workers Faculty (Arbeiter-und-Bauern-Fakultät or ABF), which was founded in 1949 to promote education up to university entrance level among working people (the system was largely run down after 1961 in the context of wider reforms in the education system). Alongside the socialist theme of post-war re-construction and its message of participation in society, the work is original for its technical use of montage and varying temporal perspectives in the narration, thus progressing beyond the more orthodox linearity commonly adopted by other exponents of social realism. Himself a worker-student of the post-war ABF which he protrays in The Auditorium, Kant became in 1978 President of the the Writers' Federation of the GDR (Schriftstellerverband der DDR), which is the official authors' umbrella organisation.

The most successful of Erwin STRITTMATTER's works has been Old Bienkopp (Ole Bienkopp, 1963), which was preceded by novels dealing primarily with recent historical subjects set in rural Germany (e.g. Tinko, published in 1954 and filmed in 1957, which depicts the land reform from a child's perspective). Old Bienkopp is the story of an individual who is determined to live his own way out of tune with the party directives and ends tragically as a result. A former local mayor and People's Correspondent, Strittmatter became in 1959 first secretary to the Writers' Federation of the GDR and thereafter a Vice-President.

In his lyric poetry and narrative prose Stephan HERMLIN's favoured subjects lie in the Nazi period and the resistance to it both within Germay and beyond. Thus already in Lieutenant Yorck von Wartenburg (1946) the subject is an officer who is condemmed to death after the attempt on Hitler's life on the 20th July 1944, while The Time of Community (Die Zeit der Gemeinsamkeit, 1949) protrays the insurrection by the Jews in the Warsaw Ghetto. Hermlin is, moreover, a prolific and non-dogmatic publicist, critic, translator and editor who has shown himself to be keenly interested in world trends beyond those cultivated within the GDR.

In 1965 at a plenary conference of the Central Committee of the SED, Erich Honecker (who would succeed Ulbricht as party leader some years later) gave a report of the Politbureau which was heavily critical of output in all areas of cultural activity on the grounds that the depiction of supposed mistakes and failures in the organisation of the state were spreading scepticism among the population and undermining morale.[30] In particular certain films came under attack alongside the singer, Wolf Biermann, the writer, Stefan Heym and the scientist, Professor Robert Havemann.

Stefan HEYM, who had emigrated to the USA during the war and returned as an American soldier, was dismissed from the US Army for his pro-communist views and settled in the GDR in 1952. In novels, publications and plays, he considers historical and contemporary issues, such as 19th century socialism, American policy, Stalinism and the workers' revolt of the 17th June 1953. His novel of the 17th June, however, was not published in East Germany (it could only appear in the Federal Republic in 1974), while Ahasver (1979) is critical of the dangers of atomic warfare and of bureaucratism. In 1979 Heym was expelled from the Writers' Federation and his works could only appear in the West.

Wolf BIERMANN proved to be the centre of extreme and far-reaching controversy for the cultural politicians of the GDR. From a working family whose father was murdered in Auschwitz concentration camp, he moved to the GDR in 1953 and studied philosophy and mathematics. In 1963 he was expelled from the SED, however, and suffered a general prohibition on either publishing or performing his songs. In 1976 the GDR deprived him of East German citizenship (i.e. he was deported) and he moved first to Hamburg and in 1982 to Paris. His songs progressed from mild and constructive criticism of the system in the GDR to either aggressive negation or resigned scepticism. Particular targets for him were bureaucracy, the Stalinist perversion of socialism and authoritarianism. Not limiting himself to conditions in the GDR, however, he expressed solidarity with numerous democratic-socialist efforts and movements throughout the world.

Alongside Biermann, Robert HAVEMANN, became something of a mouthpiece and leader of the intellectual socialist opposition to the dictatorial-bureaucratic version of communism as practised by the SED. A communist party member since 1932 and condemned to death under the Nazis for resistance activities, he nonetheless survived the fascist period and the war to become Professor of Chemistry at the Humboldt University in East Berlin (1964) and member of the People's Chamber (1950-1963). Recipient of the GDR's National Prize in 1959, he was a clear opponent of the SED from 1956 until his death in 1982. In 1966 he lost his professional position as director of a scientific institute in Berlin and was expelled from the national Academy of Sciences the same year. So intense was the ideological battle after 1965 that, for a short while, the SED even enjoined its scientists and technocrats to spurn the results of research work and developments in the West in its attempt to seal the country off from contact with the capitalist world.[31] By this stage there had been numerous artistic dissidents and figures who did not conform to the ideological groove in the cultural history of the GDR. The author Gerhard ZWERENZ, who had been associated with the oppositional Harich-Group, was forced to flee to West Berlin in 1957, while the documentary playwright Heinar KIPPHARDT returned to West Germany in 1959 and the lyricist and short story writer Christa REINIG did not return to the East from a visit in the West during 1964 since her work had remained unpublished in the GDR since 1951. In 1962 the poet Peter HUCHEL, for whom an important theme was the relationship between nature and the world of work, lost his post as chief editor of the literary periodical _Sinn_ _und_ _Form_ on account of his alleged ideological unsoundness, and remained under publisher's prohibition until repeated requests to leave the GDR were granted in 1971.

9.5 1971: A Thaw in Cultural Policy

The general ideological position on cultural affairs as established at the Bitterfeld Conference and by the SED from 1965 persisted until Ulbricht's demise in 1971. The new leader, Erich Honecker, if anything introduced a new political and ideological purism in contrast to his predecessor and the commitment to social realism as the model for the artist in the GDR was re-affirmed. At the 8th Party Congress in 1971, however, the SED signified its approval for a certain widening of stylistic horizons beyond those which had predominated for so long. The dawn of a new pluralism and of a creative cultural debate among artists was announced by the Central Committee between 1972 and 1973, when Honecker stated that socialist art could proceed from a variety of themes and styles and that the spectrum of creativity could be broader and more colourful than hitherto.[32] As a direct result some previously forbidden works could now become available.

The early 1970s were an especially productive and exciting phase in the cultural history of East Germany, which was marked by bold literary experiments on the themes of bourgeois convention and the conflict between individual happiness and the social process.

The most successful and talked-about theatrical production of this period was Ulrich PLENZDORF's The New Sufferings of Young W (Die Neuen Leiden des Jungen W, 1972), which echoed problems of young people in the GDR in its representation of the 17-year old apprentice, Edgar Wibeau, who cannot integrate himself into the conventional process of work and training and finally loses his life during the construction of a new production-boosting facility at his plant.

Similar conflicts for the individual within a political straightjacket are found in the prose and poetry of Volker BRAUN, who demands satisfaction of human needs in the face of the monotony of work and a cynical and selfish bureaucracy: Braun's socialism is one which is constantly striving for the good of the human being in a state of permanent evolution or even "revolution".

Further figures who contributed to this period of experimentation and social critique centred on the problems of the individual include the writers Günter de BRUYN and Brigitte REIMANN (e.g. in Franziska Linkerhand, 1974), Klaus SCHLESINGER and Rolf SCHNEIDER.

9.6 1976: An End to Flexibility

From 1971 to 1976 the government pursued a relatively liberal cultural policy. This came to an abrupt end, however, in 1976, when the state began to react once again to suppress voices of criticism and destabilisation. The immediate cause of this reaction was, not only the usual problems of economic backwardness in relation to the expectations of a population constantly comparing their own standard of living with that of the West

Germans, but also, at this particular time, the somewhat unexpected effects of the international debate on human rights which had been provoked by the Helsinki agreements, to which both the GDR and the USSR were signatories.

It is also essential to understand the particular role which literature and art fulfil in a society which is highly controlled and censored and for which neither the media nor oppositional political parties provide any genuine forum for criticism of the state. This forum, which is naturally provided for in the West, exists in the East only in terms of permitted art and literature. Not surprisingly, therefore, even ordinary citizens in the GDR look to their authors, poets and playwrights for any significant debate about life and conditions in their own country, rather more so, certainly, than the inhabitants of the West, for whom most intellectual art remains a remote and highbrow activity. The politicisation of literary art in East Germany, which is a product of the SED's monopoly, in turn leads to it becoming a focus of opposition and a target for recurrent cultural censorship: thus, ironically, the points are set for future repression precisely at periods of relative liberalisation.

9.7 The Biermann-Protest

An open crisis was provoked in 1976 by the deprivation of GDR citizenship of the dissident singer, Wolf Biermann, which was followed by that of the poet and writer, Reiner Kunze, the following year. The actual protest was unprecedented in the history of the GDR for its scale and the solidarity it revealed among the cultural community. An unpolemical and restrained document, it was signed by over a hundred artists within the GDR who pleaded for a certain tolerance of uncomfortable views within the context of responsible and critical analysis of contemporary society. The protest was not signed by Hermann Kant, Peter Hacks or Anna Seghers, who, on the other hand, made a restrained announcement on the issue. The immediate reaction of the authorities was obvious irritation, although, in terms of policy, attempts were made to avoid direct conflict by reference to the need for a deeper understanding of the particular situation of the GDR: i.e. as a young socialist country at an early stage of historical and cultural evolution and still in conflict with a hostile and imperialist West Germany. Despite the acknowledgment of the necessity of constructive criticism, however, it was stressed that art and literature were expected to adopt a more apologistic role and affirm socialism more positively.

In practice many of those who openly protested against the expulsion of Biermann experienced official pressure, arrest, encouragement to leave the GDR or even subsequent deportation to the Federal Republic. Protesters included the poets Bernd Jentzsch, Sarah Kirsch and Hans-Joachim Schädlich, as well as the novelist Jurek Becker. Becker was a former SED-member since 1957 who was expelled from the party for his Biermann-protest in 1976 but left the Writers' Federation the following year of his own accord. A favourite theme of Becker's novels is the - autobiographical - experience of the wartime Ghetto and the Nazi concentration camp (Jacob the Liar (Jakob der Lügner), 1969 and The Boxer (Der Boxer), 1976), although in Leading Astray the Authorities (Die Irreführung der Behörden, 1973) the personal problems of a writer coping with official success and recognition in the GDR are described, while Sleepless Days (Schlaflose Tage), 1978, portrays a teacher who takes the radical step of leaving his wife and his job out of a general sense of frustration at conformity. In 1977 Becker left to live in West Berlin with the permission of the GDR.

Not all artists left the GDR willingly, although they and their families were subjected to official persecution and psycholgocial terror tactics. In the immediate years following the aftermath of the Biermann-protest, several continued to leave East Germany in the cultural crackdown . These included Karl-Heinz Jackobs, Günter Kunert, Erich Loest, Klaus Poche, Klaus Sschlesinger, Rolf Schneider and Joachim Seyppel. Stefan Heym left in 1979, while Christa Wolf continued to publish, taking advantage of the more open reception to stylistic innovations which was heralded in 1971. This is evident in her anthology of short stories, Under the Lime Trees (Unter den Linden, 1974), in which romantic-phantastic elements are used, while in No Place. Nowhere (Kein Ort. Nirgendwo), a fictitious historical meeting between the romantic writers Heinrich von Kleist and Karoline von Günderode, who both committed suicide, is the setting to explore the problems of the contemporary author. The complex and wide-ranging autobiographical novel Model of Childhood (Kindheitsmuster, 1976) treats the problems of a current generation which grew up under fascism, and the short story Cassandra (Kassandra, 1983) considers the woman's experience of historical events and the threat of the destruction of humanity through nuclear war.

The concern with international peace which writers in both East and West Germany share was highlighted by an inter-German conference, organised by Stephan Hermlin with the approval of Erich Honecker, on the theme of support for world peace ("Berliner Begegnung zur Friedensförderung"). This took place in 1981 and attracted leading cultural figures from the Federal Republic and the GDR, including the - for the East Germans - persona non grata, Stefan Heym and Jurek Becker. Heym was outspoken in his criticism of both Soviet and American positions on the arms race, on their stationing of foreign missiles in Europe and on wars of intervention, which were not a monopoly of either one side or the other. No doubt such a clear and neutralist position could not be echoed by those still living and working in the GDR, but the conference was successful in raising key international issues and in demonstrating the considerable measure of cultural unity of German intellectuals in the face of political division.

9.8 Cultural Opportunites for the People

In general terms the GDR can be proud of the ways in which efforts have been made to give ordinary people inexpensive access to cultural pursuits and events. Book production increased between 1950 and 1980 from 4 to 9.1 books per head of population, with a high rate of actual purchase and consumption of non-trivial literature. Numbers visiting museums of art, moreover, doubled between 1965 and 1980..[33] Within a national programme of cultural promotion and support, "Creative Artistic Activity among the People" (künstlerisches Volksschaffen), it was estimated in 1978 that over one and half million working citizens were engaged in some cultural activity of one form or another, of these perhaps 600,000 in about 25,000 collectives specifically established for this purpose and bringing together professional artists and amateurs. The activities themselves encompass writing, drama, cabaret, film, dance, applied and pure arts, handicrafts and music, etc., and where appropriate involving children as well as adults. The groups themselves may be located at places of work as well as in clubs and "Houses of Culture" located in both town and village.

Since 1972 a National Workers Festival (Arbeiterfestspiele der DDR) is held every two years (annually between 1959 and 1971) in a different local region (Bezirk) of the the GDR. The festival presents a large range of cultural activities and events from home and from other socialist countries, for which collectives prepare performances and contributions which are finally selected by competition. Prizes are awarded and professional artists assist with the preparation.

9.9 The Cultural Underground

"The Alternative" is a term commonly used within West Germany to denote a section of mainly youthful members of society who have opted out of conventional patterns of living, working and achieving success and who identify themselves strongly with anti-authoritarian attitudes and patterns of living. In recent years in East Germany, too, an increasing number of individuals have identified themselves with a free, largely underground culture, which disavows the inherited and strongly propagated values of their socialist state. The price of opting out in this way can be high in the GDR, but its centre is in the run-down quarter of Prenzlauer Berg in East Berlin, where pre-war slums are still to be found. Poetry readings, exhibitions and rock concerts are the cultural expressions of this movement, which is quietly tolerated by the state as long as it remains unobtrusive. Sascha Anderson, a song-writer and poet from this scene, who was allowed to leave the GDR in August 1986, claims that there exist fundamental differences between the East German alternative movement and the kind of active protest represented by Wolf Biermann. Artists like Anderson assert that they are "freer" than those of the Biermann-generation, if only because their own form of life and protest is well-established and because they represent the beginnings of a generation which has never opted for the system and hence - unlike Biermann - have no need to opt out of it. The position is interesting for a variety of reasons. It implies, not only a complete cultural disinterest in the social system of the GDR, but also, perhaps, the readiness of the state to tolerate a level of alternative culture.[34]

9.10 A Note on Dissidence

Dissidence or opposition to the government and conditions in the GDR is generally associated with cultural figures, especially writers and poets. The reason for this is clear from the particular role which culture has come to exercise in the GDR as a forum of discussion about the state. However, it is the purpose of this final section to show by way of conclusion that dissidence as such is a complex social phenomenon embracing various activities, organisations and personalities in the GDR.[35] Since power is held to be already in the hands of the working community and is used only for the common good, there can be no obective justification for opposition in a socialist state. This, at any rate, is the official view of the SED and serves to deprive any manifestation of dissidence in the GDR of genuine legitimacy. (In non-communist countries, however, opposition to the bourgeois state is approved if it emanates from the working class.) In practice, however, the SED has had to cope with varying degrees of opposition, with the limit to what it will tolerate being exceeded if constructive criticism turns into fundamentally anti-socialist attitudes. Criticism as such is encouraged in theory as long as it is for the furtherance of the party's aims and policies, and is directed, say, at lackadaisical functionaries or inefficent economic practices. With the changeover from Ulbricht to Honecker, it was acknowledged that different social strata still existed in some tension, so that the grounds for opposition to some extent became more respectable than they had been. On the other hand, with the party at the same time re-affirming the importance of ideology and its own political leadership in a community which had yet to achieve the harmony of pure socialism, the potential for crackdown actually increased.

The following major forms of current opposition in the GDR have been distinguished:[36]

(1) Intellectual Dissidents, such as Robert Havemann, Rudolf Bahro and Stefan Heym. Of these, Rudolf Bahro has recently shaken the party most of all. He was, after all, a party member and trained economist, who delivered a long-planned and carefully rehearsed public attack on the system in 1977 with the full knowledge that he would be arrested and imprisoned (sentenced to eight years, he was released to the West in 1979). Clearly his new vision of Marxism, in which, perhaps less utopian in concept than Havemann, he argued for a retention of total control but without the degrading domination of an elite over the people that continues to characterise the "ownership" of the East Germans by the SED, unnerved the GDR leadership through its very pinpointing of basically anti-socialist features of communist regimes. Common to most left-wing dissidents such as Bahro are deep dissillusionment with the SED after an often long period of active conformity, the condemnation of the communist party's preoccupation with the pursuit of economic wealth in its effort to outdo capitalism, a scepticism of archaic and anarchical conditions in the West, and a belief in

true Marxist socialism as yet unrealised in Eastern Europe.

(2) Those who "vote with their feet". As many as 3% of the GDR's citizens just want to leave the country, mainly to enjoy a better material life in West Germany. The state's willingness to grant exit visas has not been consistent under Honecker, but, although many who experience disadvantage and persecution through their persistence in applying to leave are drawn towards acts and gestures of dissidence, these are different from the "true" dissidents inasmuch as they do not truly oppose the state in the sense that they are motivated by a political vision to change it from within: they merely wish to opt out.

(3) The peace movement. From 1978, when the state introduced compulsory pre-military training in schools for 15-16 year old children, the Evangelical Church spearheaded dissent on behalf of many young people objecting to the GDR's commitment to the international arms race and the increasing militarisation of civilian life. The climax was the Dresden Peace Forum of 1982 which was organised by the Church, attended by 5000 young East Germans, and voiced a lot of criticism of official policy. The Church further advocated community work as an alternative to service in the armed forces (a proposal which went much further than the official alternative for pacifists in the services, viz. work in non-combatant "construction units", which has existed since 1964). Although the SED firmly rejected this proposal, it, like the Church itself, has avoided direct confrontation with a moderate unofficial peace movement in order to maintain unity with the Church and to contain dissent among young citizens. Not unlike some western governments in the 1980s, however, it remains hostile to disarmament and, with unmistakeable cynicism, approves of peace movements in the West while barely tolerating its own (some activists have been imprisoned or deported). Recent years have seen a very broad and complex debate involving peace campaigners, intellectuals and writers, which links the issues of international disarmament with

human rights in the GDR itself. A symbolic focus of the conflict has been the "Swords into Ploughshares" emblem of the peace movement groups, which was banned in 1982, but re-admitted shortly afterwards.

In an assessment of the significance of opposition, Woods (1986)[37] concludes that, despite a generally low level of political interest among young East Germans and uncertainty as to just how representative dissidence expressed by intellectuals is of the wider population, the SED takes criticism very seriously and reflects major issues in its own internal discussions. These may concentrate on economic inefficiency and failures, the goals of material wealth versus human development, damage to the environment and even the emancipation of women. Regarding the role of women, it has always been official policy that freedom to work and participate in the means of social production has long liberated wives and mothers in the GDR from traditional subordination, but practice suggests that this has merely re-doubled their burden and restricted their lives even further in the light of prevailing patriarchal attitudes.

CHAPTER 10
MEDIA IN THE GDR

Article 27 of the constitution of the GDR states that "the freedom of the press, radio and television is guaranteed", which, in the official commentary, is interpreted to mean that the East German media are free to propagate the ideals and aims of Socialism and are protected from "misuse" by "bourgeois ideologies" hostile to Marxism-Leninism. The definition of the term "misuse" is in practice somewhat broad. In particular, the GDR's legal codex (Strafgesetzbuch) renders a wide range of rather diffusely defined activities as punishable offences irrespective of the context of the media; these offences can vary from the collection of news items, to incitement to war or anti- socialist propaganda and slander of the state. In other words the constitional guarantee of freedom to publish and broadcast is valid primarily for the purposes and aims of the socialist state as it exists at any specific time.

The Basic Law of the Federal Republic of Germany also contains a guarantee of freedom for press and broadcasting:

> Everyone shall have the right freely to express and disseminate his opinion by speech, writing and pictures and freely to inform himself from generally accessible sources. Freedom of the press and freedom of reporting by means of broadcasts and films are guaranteed. There shall be no censorship (Article 5)

In contrast to the GDR, then, the institutional freedom of the media in West Germany is derived from the freedom of the individual citizen. It is defined in practical terms of "access to information" and "freedom of expression" and is given no explicit ideological direction. Although the state may confiscate material after it has appeared, it has no powers of censorship before publication (and even then only a judge may order confiscation). Of utmost significance for the press in the Federal Republic is the acknowledgement in law of its so-called "public function" which, among other things, entitles it to criticise judges, legal decisions, manufacturers, politicians and the government in the general public interest. Although the West German press has experienced a number of conflicts with various interests (e.g. on the right to information from official sources, criticism of the standards of manufactured goods and the notorious Spiegel-affair,[38]) its fundamental independance as an institution with primary accountability to the public is not seriously questioned. The "public function" also requires of the media a certain legal responsibility to ensure the veracity of what is reported, although in this respect considerable reliance is placed on the newspaper concern's own advisory body, the German Press Council (Deutscher Presserat), to ensure standards of conduct. From all this it should be clear that the essence of the public function lies in the legal independance of political or economic interests. Of course, the law is one thing while the issues of private monopoly and the control of information (especially in the light of new technology) confronting West Germany today are another, but the ethos of the public function contrasts sharply with the virtual identification of state and public media in the GDR. To appreciate the nature of this identification it is necessary to explore the ideological basis on which the media of the GDR operate.

10.1 The Ideological Basis

Although, under the experience of Prussian censorship, Marx and Engels stressed the need for freedom of the press, deploring even financial or political dependancy of newspapers on the communist party, Lenin significantly redefined the role of the early communist press in a formulation which is essentially valid today:

The role of the newspaper is not, however, confined purely to the dissemination of ideas, nor to political education and winning over of political allies. The newspaper is not only a collective agitator, but also a collective organiser.[39] The major function of the press is, then, to participate in the ideological education of the people, the creation of "socialist consciousness" in the minds of the citizens, and, of course, to take a leading role in the public attack on non-communist ways of thought. As a "propagandist" it disseminates Marxist-Leninist ideology throughout all levels of the population. As "agitator" it interprets day-to-day occurrences in the light of specific aspects of this ideology and endorses party policy of the day on current or immediate issues. As "organiser" it engages actively as an agent of the state in the practical work of political, economic and cultural collectives and is expected to show tangible results in these spheres.

It is as an organiser - the role which Lenin emphasised most strongly - where the differences between communist and western media become most obvious. In the West it is generally assumed that one of the media's central functions is the politically neutral transmission of news and that this is incompatible with acting as an instrument of government policies. This conception of the neutrality of news in the West is, incidentally, rejected out of hand in Marxist-Leninist ideology as a calculated fiction. Apart from the fact that the very selection of material alone precludes completely objective reporting, "news" is felt to possess an inherent "class" character which is usually disguised in the West. For example, a news item introduced by the phrase, "The President of the USA speaks on television", entails (but does not make explicit) the information that the speaker is the representative of the leading western (= imperialist) power. Another example is the apparently innocuous statement that "the trade balance between the FRG and South Africa is favourable" which, as reported in the West, fails to make clear the important fact that West Germany is flouting official UN policy by trading with a racialist regime (whereas an East German reader would have been sufficiently pre-educated to appreciate the implications of this information, the western reader generally is not.[40] The western presentation of information is fundamentally criticised because it conceals the reality of class conflict and crisis in its own society (e.g. through the deliberate use of euphemisms such as "pluralistic society", "economic regression", "rationalisation" to conceal deep social divisions or economic crises) and also because it has developed the myth of information as a marketable commodity, a consumable product manufactured and exploited by a highly developed and profitable mass communications industry. The western consumer's apparent need for news represents in reality urges and desires implanted or suggested from outside in order to satisfy the economic needs of the media industry itself - hence the phenomenon of the sensationalist tabloid, the presentation of isolated, unconnected and often trivial items of information, and the diversionary character of much of the news content. The perspective plan for the East German News Agency (Allgemeiner Deutscher Nachrichtendienst, or ADN) for the 1960's thus contained the proposal for more overall reviews and greater depth and complexity in the presentation of news material so that items would not be seen as a haphazard collection of isolated facts but as components of a more meaningful whole. Thus it is claimed that a debate in the West German parliament, for instance, is impossible to interpret on the basis of an individual news item and requires just such a deliberate placing in the context of the capitalist system.[41] . The most important thing for the recipient of news is to draw conclusions, perceive relationships and correlate individual items with the social context. The ideological dismissal of the western media applies to the entire spectrum of non-communist news publications and even the more serious newspapers of the West are summarily categorized as "bourgeois" and as instruments of the capitalist system. Just as the bourgeois press itself arose during the nineteenth century as an instrument of political opposition on behalf of the middle classes, so is every newspaper, in East or West, held to represent necessarily the interests of a social class. As recently as 1981 this notion was affirmed by Erich Honecker at the Tenth Party Congress of the SED:

The mass media are playing an exceedingly

important role in our day. They are instruments of ideological struggle in the hands of the workers' and farmers' state and, on the other side, in the hands of the imperialist bourgeoisie.

It should not be thought, however, that the notion that the individual is encouraged to draw "objective" conclusions in any way signifies that he has the freedom to conclude what he likes. In Marxist-Leninist terms an objective assessment of social reality in the West primarily involves a recognition of the continuing class struggle there and of the exploitation of the workers in the anachronistically capitalist system. The entire educative process in the GDR, whether in school, the factory, or in reading the newspaper, is conducted in terms of the superiority of the communist world view and does not aim to offer the citizen unrestricted intellectual choice between different political or social philosophies. The West,for example, is far from neglected in terms of media coverage - there being a constant public analysis of its defects - but coverage is selective and concentrates heavily on negative aspects, such as the Berufsverbot in the FRG (by which "suspected" communists were excluded from employment in public services ranging from teaching to working on the railways), poverty in cities, race riots, Northern Ireland, etc. As we shall see below the media have developed very much as organs of the communist party, vital tools in the education and organisation of the people. No attempt is made to disguise this or to pretend that reporting is not politically slanted. And no secret is made of the censorship principle behind the selective filtering of information:

> We do not print all and everything regardlessly. Our press brings those things which serve the mass of the people. The opponent is only allowed to speak if it serves our purposes.[42]

The statute of the ADN, which is the only news agency to which East German newspapers may subscribe, was officially amended in 1966 to commit the agency exclusively to relaying political information of a socialist character.

10.2 History and Organisation of the Press

As in the Federal Republic the press in the GDR today originated in the conditions which prevailed in occupied Germany after 1945. The occupying powers issued licences for the publishing of newspapers, in the West largely to individuals, in the East primarily to organisations, viz. the approved political parties. From the start, however, the newspapers of the communist party (KPD) were given preference inasmuch as they appeared first and received an adequate supply of printing paper. After the merger of the KPD and the SPD in 1946 the official organs of the two parties also combined to form Neues Deutschland, the mouthpiece of the Socialist Unity Party (SED) on the 23rd April 1946.

1947 saw the official suspension of pre-publication censorship by the Soviet authorities, although in practice a rigorous post-publication censorship operated which could entail curtailment of the paper allocation, dismissal or even the arrest of editors.

In 1949 direct control passed from the occupying power into the hands of the SED in the form of an official agency now known as the Press Office (Presseamt). The Presseamt performs the following key functions:

- Directly responsible to the Council of Ministers (Ministerrat), it ensures that the latter's policy on news and information is carried out. The monopoly of the SED and its control of government bodies such as the Council of Ministers ensures that the effective controlling organ of the media is the relevant department of the party apparatus itself, in this case the Department for Agitation of the Central Committee of the SED.

- It publishes government communiques, organises press conferences and issues regular bulletins and commentaries on topical issues (these bulletins or

"Presseinformationen" are authoritative of official policy and are received by the media, government departments and industry).

- All newspapers require a licence in order to appear which is issued by the Press Office and may be revoked at any time. Control by licence was first employed by the occupying powers and the device as such has been retained in the GDR, although the system of recruitment, training and self- censorship is now so well established that the application of such crude techniques is superfluous. In law, however, licences may be issued to state institutions, academies, political parties, mass organisations, publishers and individuals on condition that the publication conforms to the laws of the GDR and provided that material sources for its production are available within the terms of the current economic plan. The chief editor or publisher is responsible for adhering to the terms of the licence and penalties for transgression include fines and confiscation.

The state not only controls press publications by means of the Press Office, the licence system and the allocation of resources, but also through its monopoly of the distribution and sales network. Newspapers, magazines,etc may only be legally distributed in the GDR if they are on the so-called "postal list" (Postzeitungsliste) of the East German Post Office Ministry. The subscription of western publications is strictly limited and requires special permission. Newspaper printing is the province of a holding company of the SED itself, the Zentrag (Zentrale Druckerei-, Einkaufs- und Revisionsgesellschaft mbH, founded 1945), which controls the entire newspaper and book publishing and distribution network of the GDR, even in areas not directly related to the SED itself. The Zentrag is also responsible for advertising production (through the Deutsche Werbe- und Anzeigegesellschaft mbH, founded 1946) and for the national film distribution service (Progress Film-Vertrieb). Rather more significant for the ideological function of the mass media than the bureaucratic agencies of central control is the role of Kaderpolitik, viz. the placing of expertly trained party members in key positions of such areas as administration, industry, science, education and the media. Such experts, acting both as professional leaders in their field and as ideological mentors at the place of work ensure that communist party policy is carried out as widely and effectively as possible at all levels and in all areas of life in the GDR.

Organisation by Kaderpolitik acquired great importance for the media from 1950 when the SED formulated plans for the creation of a "new type" of press and media on the Soviet model. The aim was to neutralise the remnants of the bourgeois and oppositional press and to give a unified ideological direction to all branches of the media (whereas the SED had always exerted full control over the radio and most of the press, products of the film industry had not always been unequivocally socialist in character). The new policy had been prepared by a delegation of SED editors who had visited Moscow to make a thorough study of the organisation and methods of Pravda and was implemented by means of a so-called "structural plan" according to which editorial policy of a newspaper became the overall responsibility of a five-man collective, the Redaktionskollegium. A further body, the Redaktionssekretariat, was set up on the Russian model to plan current issues in advance and to co-ordinate the activities of the various departments according to the overall plan. The secretariat was made responsible for each issue and provided the backbone of the efficiently run communist newspaper. The two most important individual departments envisaged in the structural plan dealt with "party life" and propaganda respectively. The former (again modelled on Pravda) consisted of experienced party functionaries and became responsible for the day-to-day ideological training of party members. The dissemination of Marxist-Leninist ideology became the task of the department for propaganda, which also supported the campaigns for party membership and the political education programmes. Further departments included economy, culture, sport, readers' letters, "people's correspondents" (see below), etc.

The "new press" of 1950 was not just restructured internally but also integrated into the national system of long term economic planning. Walter Ulbricht made it clear that it was no longer sufficient for a newspaper to construct its copy on the basis of day-to-day events and that journalists faced the loftier task of working within a planned socialist system. The procedures introduced as a result laid the foundations of a style of ideological journalism which characterises the East German press to this day. Following general directives from the Department of Agitation and Propaganda of the Central Committee of the SED and from the Press Office, directives which are themselves co-ordinated to the national plan, individual newspapers work out quarterly plans for news themes and presentations which are submitted for central party approval. On the basis of the quarterly plans the newspapers themselves draw up monthly and weekly plans. Given the system of long-term planning and submission and also the fact that newspapers may only take their news material from the ADN (which is subject to the directives of the Council of Ministers) external post-publication censorship by the government is unnecessary.

The themes that are fixed for the coming quarter or month may include such topics as the Month of Soviet-German Friendship, activation programmes for certain sections of the economy, refugees from the FRG, East-West German agreement on passes for the Berlin Wall, community self-help initiatives for the renovation of school buildings or a West German Army general with a Nazi background. Articles on these themes will then appear, perhaps even daily, for the period of the plan. The various departments will co-ordinate their contributions accordingly: thus the economic department decides which factory it will spotlight in the preparations for the Month of Soviet Friendship, the agricultural department will prepare an article on harvesting procedure in the Soviet Union, and so on. A striking example of an extremely well-orchestrated theme co-ordinated across the press, the broadcasting media and the cinema occurred during 1979/80. The occasion was the liberation of

Germany from the Nazis by the Red Army thirty five years earlier and saw cycles of war films shown on TV and in the cinemas, a twenty-part Soviet television serial about the war on the Eastern Front, as well as documentaries, eye-witness reports and accounts by soldiers and military leaders. The purpose of the media campaign, which was backed up by a variety of activities in the mass organisations, especially those concerned with youth, was to extol the heroism of the Soviet Army, particularly at a time when its image needed refurbishing after the invasion of Afghanistan.

The central planning system undoubtedly leads to wide-spread uniformity and monotony in the headlines, commentaries and presentation of news material throughout the country (articles and speeches originating in the Soviet Union may be quoted at length). Apart from the fact that certain events may be, at least for a period, deliberately ignored by the media (such as unrest in Poland or the activities of the Peace Movement in East Germany itself), a further consequence is that newspapers are not usually able to respond quickly to unforeseen events and that readers may have to wait several days before they are reported (because the failure of public services to cope with the severe winter of 1978/9 went largely unmentioned the population was unable to prepare itself for hardship). The East German media, however, attach little significance to the speedy transmission of news in the western fashion and are willing to accept delay for the sake of uniformity.

10.3 Structure of the Press

In spite of their ideological conformity newspapers and journals are not intended to be exactly alike. In 1959 Kurt Blecha of the Press Office stressed the need for each publication to develop its individual appeal and to tailor ideology to its own type of readership. Thus the press should appeal to the various sections of the population in different ways and lead them to the same goal. The structure of the press in the GDR reflects this aim, almost all newspapers being either organs of political parties or of mass organisations. In the centrally planned system the number of newspapers and the structure of the press has not changed significantly in the last twenty years.

The SED party press easily dominates in terms of size of circulation and is responsible for: Neues Deutschland: Zentral- organ des ZK der SED (daily circulation over 1m in 1982); Neue Deutsche Zeitung: Organ des ZK der SED (weekly, over 163 000 in 1980); Einheit: Zeitschrift für Theorie und Praxis des wissenschaftlichen Sozialismus (monthly, 257,800 in 1980); Neuer Weg: Organ des ZK der SED für Fragen des Parteilebens (fortnightly, 205,000 in 1980). The SED also brings out the so-called "works newspapers" (Betriebszeitungen) for the party organisations in the larger organisations in the larger branches of work, industry and state institutions such as the universities (fortnightly, c. 2.5 m; 657 titles in 1982). Workers contribute to the copy and production of these newspapers and receive material rewards. According to polls and questionnaires the Betriebszeitungen are among the most popular and widely read of news publicatons. At the district level, the SED produces daily a local Bezirkszeitung, one for each of the 15 districts and each with its own title (e.g. Leipziger Volkszeitung, Sächsische Zeitung, Berliner Zeitung, BZ am Abend). The circulation of the district SED newspapers was 5 million in 1981.

The so-called bourgeois parties in the GDR also publish their own newspapers and journals but since these parties acknowledge by statute the leading role of the SED and the goals of communism, the possibility of significant deviation from SED policy does not arise. These publications are directed at those sections of the population which are, in the SED's view, still politically backward and they are intended to function essentially as instruments of re-education in the continuing debate with opposing ideologies. Der Morgen (circulation 50,900) is the organ of the LDPD and is aimed at the middle social strata (shop owners, professional people, etc) while Neue

Zeit (86100) (CDUD) looks at issues from a Christian point of view. The central organ of the NDPD, the Nationalzeitung (58,800), was founded in 1948 in order to win over former members of the Nazi party and army officers for the communist government. In comparison to the breadth of circulation of the SED's own press, that of the minor parties is small fry: of the regional dailies, for example, the CDUD puts out only 5, the LDPD 4, the NDPD 5. In addition the other parties produce monthly journals for party members and officials, e.g. Union teilt mit (CDUD), Der nationale Demokrat (NDPD). A further party, the Demokratische Bauernpartei Deutschlands, which was founded in 1948 with very close ties with the SED, is concerned with the interests of farm workers. Its daily newspaper is Bauern-Echo (circulation 91,100 in 1981) and the monthly for party functionaries is Der Pflüger.

The press of the mass organisations complements that of the national parties inasmuch as it pursues the ideological education of the people down to the level of a particular organised activity. One consequence of this is that it is easier from these publications to see the relationship between ideology and real life in the GDR. Examples include the numerous publications of the FDJ and youth organisations, such as Junge Welt (daily, circulation 1.1 million in 1981), Junge Generation, Pionierleiter (44,300 in 1980), Forum (for students), Neues Leben (55,800 in 1980). Trade Unions, sport and paramilitary organisations and the armed services also have a variety of journals, as well as journalists, artist, authors, etc. Of illustrated magazines, the weekly FF-dabei (for TV and radio programmes) is the most popular with a circulation of 1.4 million in 1981. The weekly Wochenpost (1.2 million in 1981) is for family consumption and contains articles and features on culture, entertainment and leisure activities as well as political reviews on both East and West. Für Dich (weekly, 900,000 in 1981) is a fifty-page magazine aimed at women; apart from articles on bringing up children, fashion, and serialised stories, etc. It too, contains political commentaries. Both Wochenpost and Für Dich are considered "important political weekly journals" by the SED.

10.4 Journalists

A look at the profession of journalism highlights the different conceptions of the role of the press in East and West. In West Germany there is no single way of becoming a reporter. In practice, would-be journalists can either spend two years in practical training (<u>Volontariat</u>) or attend one of the special schools for journalism in the Federal Republic. A further option is study at university in a subject such as economics, social sciences or media studies (<u>Publizistik</u>), although most journalists never complete their course before starting work. The general feeling seems to be that journalism is a field in which it is difficult and unwise to prescribe formal theoretical training.[43] In the GDR, by way of contrast, journalistic training is centralised at the Faculty of Journalism (<u>Sektion für Journalistik</u>) of the University of Leipzig, where during a course lasting four years (or, since 1965 on an initiative of the SED, three years following a compulsory two-year apprenticeship in a newspaper office) aspiring journalists learn the fundamentals of "socialist journalism" as a branch of the Marxist-Leninist based social sciences. Ideology constitutes the core of the course and the journalist is first and foremost trained as a skilled organiser of people and an active propagandist of communism (in 1974 a new course in techniques of oral persuasion - <u>mündliche Argumentation</u> - was incorporated into the syllabus).

The journalist in the GDR is in many respects more a party functionary than a reporter and he also fulfils external duties (e.g. speaking at a local factory) which are more in keeping with a representative of the government than we should normally associate with a journalist in the West.

Special mention should be made of the "people's correspondents" (<u>Volkskorrespondenten</u>), a movement which was initiated in 1948 on the Soviet model of selecting and training workers from industry, agriculture and other organisations to contribute regularly to a newspaper (GDR radio also participates in the scheme). After disappointing results the movement was re-vitalised in the 1960's and there are now about 20,000 such correspondents in the country, working mainly with local newspapers. They report on their own sphere of work and assume an organising role in the fulfilment of economic targets. Not all their reports are published and many serve just to provide information for government departments.

The professional organisation for journalists is the Verband der Journalisten der DDR (VDJ), which was founded in 1946 (then: Verband der deutschen Presse) and has belonged to the national trade union federation (FDGB) since 1953. Its chairman is Central Committee candidate member Eberhard Heinrich (since 1981) and the organisation comprised 84000 members in 1982, over half of whom were press journalists and 18% with TV and radio.

The VDJ is well organised, with 5-yearly congresses, a central board, a presidium and its own secretariat. It is represented throughout the country, down to individual editorial offices and publishers and has recently (1982) set up commissions to improve aspects of professional journalism in the GDR (training, exchange of information, international contacts, the management of works newspapers, etc). Since 1982 it has concentrated on recruiting suitable candidates in newspaper offices for university training.

10.5 Radio

Broadcasting services in the GDR are controlled centrally by so-called State Committees (one each for radio and television) which, rather like the Presseamt, are organs of the Council of Ministers. The chairmen of the two committees are very powerful individuals, being appointed by the Council of Ministers and answerable to it for the committee's policies. In 1971 Rudolf Singer became chairman of the State Committee for Radio: a former chief editor of Neues Deutschland, he was also a member of the SED Central Committee - a sign of the political importance of the post and of the close connection between party and media. Since 1980 Achim Becker, formerly member of the Commission for The Committee for Agitation, responsible to the Politbureau, has filled the position. The State Committee for Radio determines central planning policy, draws up yearly plans and decides how the various channels are to carry them out. It further maintains close links with the radio services of other communist countries and handles all foreign broadcasting contacts. The two main radio stations in the GDR are Radio DDR I and Radio DDR II. The former transmits 24 hours a day (since 1969) and broadcasts general entertainment with hourly news bulletins; there are regular political programmes, mostly of magazine format and the main programme is supplemented by eleven regional channels. Radio DDR II is the more "serious" channel, offering cultural entertainment (concerts, plays, etc) and providing many educational programmes (including radio for schools). Political education is well represented and there is a special series, Studio 70, which deals with political ideology. Radio DDR I is the only channel to broadcast regional programmes. Directed mainly at listeners in West Germany is the Stimme der DDR (Deutschlandsender up till 1971). Broadcasting 24 hours a day it provides information and propaganda about the GDR, its foreign policy, and also about other socialist countries and foreign communist parties. One of its stated aims is the support of West German workers in their "fight for social justice". Similarly Radio Berlin International: die Stimme der DDR für das Ausland transmits in various languages throughout the world, co-ordinating its target countries with other Eastern Block states. Of further interest is the Sondersender für Gastarbeiter in der Bundesrepublik which specialises in communist programmes for foreign workers in West Germany. Two stations that are now defunct are

Deutscher Freiheitssender 904 and the Deutscher
Soldatensender 935. The Freiheitssender began
transmissions one day after the prohibition of the
communist party in the FRG in 1956 and operated until
1970 as the organ of the banned party, including in its
programmes encoded directives to party members and
couriers. From 1960 to 1972 the Soldatensender broadcast
propaganda to soldiers in the Bundeswehr.

Since West German radio and TV stations are easily
accessible to most GDR citizens, the broadcasting media
in the East do not enjoy the captive audiences of the
communist press. This competition is seen as a key aspect
of the "ideological class struggle" in view of the large
numbers of East Germans from all levels and walks of life
who tune into western stations, either for entertainment or
in order to fill the information gap (ironically the average
GDR citizen is better informed about the West than his
western counterpart is about life in the East). Attempts
to discourage the tuning in to western stations have had
little success and nowadays the widespread jamming of
radio transmissions is rare (or, at least, was so until the
Polish crisis of 1980). Tuning in to western stations has
never been a crime as such in the GDR, although the
dissemination of information from the West and listening
in groups has been subject to punishmment: regular
listening has been regarded by the state as meriting
additional punishment for other political offences. But
although East German leaders seem resigned to making a
virtue out of necessity and stress the freedom of their
citizens to choose between East and West stations.[44] this
does not mean that the struggle for audiences has been
abandoned. The 1960's State Committee for Radio
established a special section for "sociological research" to
investigate listener's tastes and the appeal of the media.
As a result recent years (especially since 1983) have seen
a concerted restructuring of programmes and channels
aimed at halting the defection of audiences to the West.
Although programmes on current political affairs are
considered to have pride of place in the broadcasting
schedule (76 news programmes are broadcast daily on the
home network), there is now more early morning

entertainment (to coincide with a peak listening period), music interspersed with news items and even introduced into political programmes, and there are more magazine programmes along western lines. A particular effort has been made to attract young listeners whose susceptibility to western entertainment, especially music, has long remained a cause of official concern. In 1972, for example, a new magazine programme for youth was created lasting from about 3 p.m. till 9 p.m. and shared across the major channels. Across all channels music now comprises two thirds of the output. Innovations of this kind in no way represent an officially acknowledged departure from the original ideological function of the media but are designed to increase and refine the effectiveness of political agitation.

10.6 Television

Much of what has been said about radio applies to television as well. As the most popular form of entertainment in the GDR its importance is highly rated by the SED, which sees it as providing a "unity of information, entertainment and education".[45] Again, information is presented selectively in news programmes with special emphasis on the sound commentary which is officially regarded as indispensable for making explicit the vital ideological conclusions emerging from the visual material: "political agitation through facts" remains the motto. The State Committee for Television, which is directly responsible to the Council of Ministers, is chaired by a Central Committee member, Heinz Adameck.

The main channel of the Fernsehen der DDR (Deutscher Fernsehfunk till 1972), the I. Programm, provides a selection of programmes for most of the day and evening ranging from daily news and education to sport, drama, children's programmes and entertainment of all kinds (popular music, serials, shows, quiz programmes, magazines, etc). There is also a brief product-advertising spot (10 minutes). The second channel or II. Programm, inaugurated in 1969, along with colour television, broadcasts in the evenings and concentrates on documentaries, educational programmes, TV films, drama, opera and concerts. It relies heavily on films and serials from the Soviet Union and other communist countries. Selected programmes from Program I are often shown on channel II, too, as is the main thirty-minute news magazine, Aktuelle Kamera.

The general public do not have access to videorecorders and there is no Teletext service. Of particular interest in the context of the East-West confrontation is the series, Der schwarze Kanal, a regular 20-minute programme conducted by the leading East German television commentator, Karl Eduard von Schnitzler, which presents a negative picture of the Federal Republic through selective presentation of West German TV material. In 1973, when the series was in its 14th year, von Schnitzler explained that the programme's role was to "unmask the methods of the capitalist mass media through the example of the Federal Republic of Germany".[46] A further programme, Alltag im Westen, also aims to keep viewers informed about life in the West through official East German eyes.

As we have observed the SED attaches utmost significance to the integration of entertainment and ideological education in the television service. How this is managed in practice, however, is a matter of some concern for the state planners. There are, of course, programmes of a purely political nature (e.g. Der schwarze Kanal) and those affording popular entertainment (Schlager Studio, Familiendisko). These complement one another possibly by virtue of sheer contrast, but otherwise can have little in common. Ideologically neutral programmes may include those on science, foreign languages or serious music, but it must be remembered that many areas of life in the GDR are politicized to a degree difficult to imagine in the West and that this is reflected in how activities are presented in the media. Competitive team sport in particular is portrayed as an essential part of socialist life, but even a Sunday performance by a children's choir can become an affirmation of the state:

"I know a beautiful land, I should like to live there for ever!..." is not only the line of of a song from the rich repertoire of the Berlin Radio Children's Choir, but also a declaration of faith. The 22-year-old artistic life of this choir is closely linked to the development of our GDR. Social commitment and artistic perfection are inseparable for these young singers. (As advertised on the 30th April 1979 - translated DL)

Where television can be both entertaining and instructive is the television play or "Spielfilm", as produced at the national film studios of the GDR, the DEFA (Deutsche Filmgesellschaft m.b.H). As a genre this has been highly promoted in the GDR and is directed at youthful audiences as well as adults. Themes, especially in the 1950's and 1960's, included Germany's Nazi past, the war and the struggle against fascism, the history of the workers' movement and adaptations of historical material, although more recently the focus has shifted to include life and problems in the contemporary GDR and dramatisations of contemporary literature. GDR television offers approximately 100 of its own drama productions every year (out of a total requirement of 500 to 600).

As in most western countries the GDR is unable to produce all its own television material and relies strongly on films and series, both ideological and non-political (e.g. detective and adventure series, comedies, etc), from other socialist countries such as the Soviet Union, Poland, Czechoslovakia and Bulgaria. Western material (mainly from USA, Britain and France) goes towards meeting the demand for entertainment (and indeed such programmes enjoy high audience ratings), although the exposure of viewers to non-communist environments is perturbing to the SED. The party has, however, openly admitted that this situation is unavoidable, stressing the urgent need for films which propagate socialism.[47] Once again direct competition with West German television has compelled the GDR to make concessions to viewers' tastes and explains the evidently strongly felt need for corrective series like Der schwarze Kanal and Alltag im Westen. The SED has in fact tried several times using members of the Free German Youth to remove aerials pointing westwards and there are regulations prohibiting communal antennae directed to West Germany, but such measures have never been effective.

An area in which East German television has been able to capture audiences from the West is in children's programmes. According to investigations by a group at the University of Tübingen in West Germany, the reasons for the success of the GDR in this field lie primarily in the fact that the East German productions have consciously integrated the child's world with everyday reality, e.g. at school, family home, the world of work, etc, whereas the West Germans, especially in the 1950's and 1960's, represented the child's world as something quite remote from the life he was actually leading. Even today, the approaches of the two countries are significantly different: West German children's programmes concentrate more on the child's free-time and his leisure activities in the afternoons, while in the GDR there is greater emphasis on life at school, in the collective and on social responsibilities. In both East and West Germany, perhaps, there is a notable failure to achieve an imaginative portrayal of the child's true needs and too strong a tendency to subordinate the child's psyche to the objective, material world and superficial social myths.[48]

10.7 Conclusion

The foregoing account has tried to draw a balanced and overall picture of the media in the GDR and above all to give some idea of how their role is understood in the country itself. It is obvious that the unique situation of direct competition with West German television has produced wide differences between the press and the broadcasting services. For a westerner the press remains drab and predictable, although East German television now often produces material of a high quality, even when it is ideologically motivated. It is hard to see what changes, if any, the future will bring (criticism of stereotyped language and political formulae in newspapers has not yet produced any significant changes). Recent studies in the GDR suggest that its people resent the information gap, especially in the portrayal of the West,[49] and would also like more entertainment. Researchers stress the need for an integrated media policy which takes account of the differences between press and radio/TV as instruments of communication: whereas television creates more immediate but also fleeting impressions, the press is better suited to developing ideas in depth. All this, of course, has implications for techniques of ideological education, but will not necessarily produce the kind of programme that will compete with the western media. Not all the results of internal surveys and research are made available, however, and there is some evidence that they may not correspond with the SED's policies or expectations.[50]

CHAPTER 11
A REVIEW OF RESOURCES

Useful general introductions in English on the GDR are provided by the following:

David Childs, The GDR: Moscow's German Ally, George Allen & Unwin, London, 1983

David Childs (ed.), Honeckers's Germany, Allen and Unwin, London, 1985.

Kurt Sontheimer, The Government and Politics of East Germany, Hutchinson, London, 1975. A dated but still informative and well presented work.

Stanley Radcliffe, 25 Years On. The Two Germanies 1970, Harrap, London, 1972.

M. McCauley, The German Democratic Republic since 1945 (Studies in Russia and East Europe), 1986.

The material in German is considerable, but comprehensive, practical and readily available studies of a more general nature include:

H. Zimmermann, H. Ulrich, M. Fehlauer, DDR Handbuch, Cologne 1985. Published by the West German Institute for Pan-German affairs, this is probably the most comprehensive compendium on all aspects of the GDR. It is in two volumes and its entries are organized alphabetically. Not apparently available in bookshops, it is distributed to educational institutions in the UK.

H. Weber, Geschichte der DDR, DTV, Munich, 1985. Excellent general and historical description of the GDR, especially its political development and apparatus up to the 1970's.

D. Staritz, <u>Geschichte</u> <u>der</u> <u>DDR</u>, Suhrkamp, Frankfurt/Main, 1985. A very informative history of the GDR which explains more fully than Weber's work the functioning of the economy and is more "up-to-date" in terms of what is happening in the 1980s.

Studies of specific aspects of the GDR, such as education and the media, are referred to in the main text of this book, but the following are worth mentioning as works of reference:

D. Gohl, <u>Deutsche Demokratische Republik. Eine aktuelle Landeskunde</u>, Fischer, 1986. A compendium of geographical and topographical information.

Karl Eckart: <u>DDR</u>, Ernst Klett Verlag, Stuttgart, 1984. A geography textbook on the GDR, covering the historical economic restructuring of the country as well as reviewing such areas as town planning, transport and foreign trade. Contains many maps and diagrams.

Hans Georg Lehmann, <u>Chronik der DDR: 1945 bis heute</u>, Verlag C. H. Beck, Munich, 1986. A handy overview of dates and events.

H. Weber (ed), <u>DDR: Dokumente zur Geschichte der Deutschen Demokratischen Republik 1945 - 1985</u>, DTV, Munich, 1986. Recommended for those interested in documents of a mainly historical and political nature pertaining to the period of the creation of the Soviet Zone of Occupation up to the GDR of the mid-1980s.

A useful series of articles and studies of various aspects of the GDR appears under the title <u>Studies in GDR Culture and Society</u>, edited by Margy Gerber and published by the University Press of America in New York and London. Six volumes have appeared to date, the contents of which are the proceedings of symposia on the

GDR, held in New Hampshire, USA.

A series of critical but informative booklets by the West German Foundation, Friedrich-Ebert-Stiftung, is published under the title DDR - Realitäten - Argumente. These are available from the foundation itself at 53 Bonn-Bad Godesberg 1, Kölner Strasse 149, Federal Republic of Germany.

A comprehensive bibliography of published material on East Germany is: East Germany, Ian Wallace (ed.), Clio Press, Oxford, 1987. Annotations for each publication are given for subject areas such as the people and its country, history, politics, religion, dissent, sport, etc. The annotations aim to be concise, informative, occasionally critical, but above all to give the reader a flavour of the issues covered by the publication.

Of periodicals, the GDR Monitor is the sole UK publication dealing exclusively with East German affairs. Most of its articles are concerned with literary topics but the Monitor in principle covers all aspects of East German studies. It is edited and published by Professor Ian Wallace, Department of Contemporary European Studies, Loughborough University.

On a more general basis the Great-Britain-GDR Society is the officially recognised Friendship Society for the two countries and membership is open to anybody with an interest in East Germany. It organizes local groups, meetings, study tours, visits and other contacts with the GDR. It is also a good source of informative publications of GDR origin, as well as providing information on study tours and visits. Its head office is at 129, Seven Sisters Road, London N7 7QG.

Subscriptions to East German newspapers, periodicals and magazines, some of them in English, are available from the international booksellers, Collets, who specialise in East European publications.

REFERENCES

[1] Walter Ulbricht, "Party of a New Type", in On Questions of Socialist Construction in the GDR, Dresden, 1968, pp. 159-169

[2] See Wolfgang Leonhard, Die Revolution entläßt ihre Kinder, Cologne, Berlin, 1956, pp. 340ff.

[3] See K. L. Baker, R. J. Dalton and K. Hildebrandt, Germany Transformed, Harvard University Press, 1981, p. 265. This volume contains a useful review of the course and development of detente from a West German point of view.

[4] Neuer Weg 28 (1973) No. 22, pp. 1009ff

[5] Erich Honecker, Report of the Central Committee Chairman to the 9th SED Party Congress, in Erich Honecker, The German Democratic Republic, New York, 1979, p. 133.

[6] Op. cit.

[7] See Chapter 2, Article 9 of the Constitution of the GDR

[8] The Second World War, Cassell 1954, vol 6, p. 448

[9] H. Zimmermann, DDR Handbuch, Cologne, 1985, p.216

[10] For a discussion of the problems of assessing the GDR's economic performance see Arthur A. Stahnke, "Progress and the GDR Economy: GDR Economic Performance and its Measurement", in Studies in GDR Culture and Society 6, Margy Gerber (ed.), New York, 1986, pp. 1-16.

[11] The Soviet-led economic union of communist states and the European Economic Community do not officially recognise one another. Talks in 1987 between the two organisations highlighted the major differences. The EEC countries insist on being able to conduct bilateral trading agreements with individual CMEA states instead of having

to negotiate with the CMEA as a whole. In particular, however, the status of Berlin has proved a major stumbling block to mutual recognition. While the EEC asserts that West Berlin should be regarded as an integral part of the EEC (as in other Community treaties), the communist countries continue to maintain that the city's division is temporary and cannot be formalised in long-term agreements. In 1987 the EEC as a whole had a 3 billion pounds sterling trading deficit with the CMEA, exporting mainly machinery and manufactured goods and importing large quantities of fuels and raw materials, principally from the Soviet Union. An improving political climate in the USSR since the accession of Mikhail Gorbachev has, however, prompted renewed attempts to overcome over 30 years of mutual non-recognition.

[12]Kulturpolitisches Wörterbuch, Berlin (East), 1978, p. 127

[13]Kulturpolitisches Wörterbuch, op. cit., P. 702

[14]H. Weber, Geschichte der DDR, Munich, 1985, p. 308

[15]Helmut Klein, Ulrich Zückert, Learning for Living. Education in the GDR, Dresden 1980, p. 56

[16]Ibid. p. 19

[17]Ibid. p. 55

[18]Ibid. pp. 19-20

[19]See H. Zimmermann, op. cit., p. 823

[20]Ibid. p. 41

[21]Ibid. p. 56

[22]What is life like in the GDR? Living Standards and Way of Life under Socialism, Dresden 1977, pp. 96-97

[23]Ibid. p. 15

[24]Ibid. p. 33

[25]Neues Deutschland, Nos 251 and 252, 23 and 24.10.1957

[26]Reported in S. Faust, In welchem Land lebt Mephisto, Munich, 1980, pp. 36ff.

[27]Neues Deutschland, No. 247, 18/10/1957

[28]Neues Deutschland, No. 3, 3/1/1960

[29]Neues Deutschland, No. 212, 3/8/1960

[30]H. Weber, op. cit., p. 367

[31]Neues Deutschland, No. 101, 13/4/1967

[32]Erich Honecker, Report of the Politbureau to the 9th Conference of the Central Committee of the SED, Berlin (East), 1973, pp. 62ff.

[33]See Heinz Heitzer, DDR. Geschichtlicher U2berblick, 2nd Edition, Berlin (East), p. 286, and H. Weber, op. cit., p. 490

[34]Interview in Der Spiegel, No. 36, 1/9/1986, pp. 74-78.

[35]For a review and classification of recent dissidence in the GDR see Roger Woods, Opposition in the GDR under Honecker, 1971-85. An Introduction and Documentation, Hampshire, 1986.

[36]Ibid.

[37]Ibid.

[38]For a fuller description see H. Meyn, Massenmedien in der Bundesrepublik Deutschland, Berlin, 1971, pp. 16ff and 47ff.

[39]W. I. Lenin, Was tun?, Berlin, 1954, p. 17 (translation by DL)

[40] Examples from L. Bisky, Massenmedien und ideologische Erziehung der Jugend, Berlin (East), 1976. pp. 16, 30

[41] K-H. Röhr, Zeitungsinformation und Bildschirm, Leipzig, 1968, p. 132

[42] See Journalistisches Handbuch der DDR, 1976.

[43] See Meyn, op.cit., pp. 72ff

[44] Erich Honecker at the 9th Congress of the Central Committee of the SED in 1973: "The western mass media, above all the radio and television of the FRG, which anybody here can switch on or off as he chooses ...", reported in P. C. Ludz and J . Kuppe, DDR Handbuch, Cologne, 1975, p. 296

[45] The 6th Central Committee Congress of the SED, 1972

[46] Reported in P. C. Ludz and J . Kuppe, DDR Handbuch, Cologne, 1975, p. 294

[47] M. Haiduk at an SED conference in April 1973

[48] "Kindermedien in beiden deutschen Staaten", a project undertaken at the Ludwig-Uhland Institut für empirische Kulturwissenschaft der Universität Tübingen, reported in Das Parlament, No. 4, 26/1/80, p. 16

[49] Röhr, op. cit., pp. 99, 107

[50] Die Zeit, No. 22, 25/5/79, pp. 9ff